Badger GCSE Religious Studies

Key Beliefs
Ultimate Questions and Life Issues *for* AQA

Michael Keene

Notes:
BCE refers to 'Before the Common Era' and has the same meaning as BC.
CE refers to 'Common Era' and has the same meaning as AD.

Terms defined in the glossary (pages 141-144) have been set in bold throughout the book either the first time they appear or where they are discussed in detail.

Contents

Understanding the syllabus and this book — 4

Section A — Key beliefs — 5

- A.1 The origins of Buddhism (1) — 6
- A.2 The origins of Buddhism (2) — 8
- A.3 Key Buddhist teachings (1) — 10
- A.4 Key Buddhist teachings (2) — 12
- A.5 Buddhist devotion — 14
- A.6 The origins of Christianity — 16
- A.7 Key Christian beliefs (1) — 18
- A.8 Key Christian beliefs (2) — 20
- A.9 Christian worship — 22
- A.10 Holy Communion — 24
- A.11 The origins and holy books of Hinduism — 26
- A.12 Key Hindu beliefs (1) — 28
- A.13 Key Hindu beliefs (2) — 30
- A.14 Hindu worship — 32
- A.15 The origins of Islam — 34
- A.16 Key Muslim beliefs (1) — 36
- A.17 Key Muslim beliefs (2) — 38
- A.18 The origins of Judaism — 40
- A.19 Key Jewish beliefs (1) — 42
- A.20 Key Jewish beliefs (2) — 44
- A.21 The origins of Sikhism — 46
- A.22 The Guru Granth Sahib — 48
- A.23 Key Sikh beliefs — 50
- A.24 Sikh worship — 52
- A.25 Christian decision-making — 54
- A.26 Four kinds of love — 56
- A.27 Christian love and forgiveness — 58
- A.28 Jesus and forgiveness — 60
- Exam questions — 62

Section B — Questions of meaning — 63

- B.1 The existence of God — 64
- B.2 The argument from design — 66
- B.3 Experiencing God — 68
- B.4 Buddhism, Christianity, Hinduism and God — 70
- B.5 Islam, Judaism, Sikhism and God — 72
- B.6 The problem of suffering — 74

B.7	Two questions about suffering	76
B.8	Buddhism, Christianity, Hinduism and suffering	78
B.9	Islam, Judaism, Sikhism and suffering	80
B.10	Life after death	82
B.11	Buddhism, Christianity, Hinduism and life after death	84
B.12	Islam, Judaism, Sikhism and life after death	86
B.13	Life after death and living today	88
	Exam questions	90

Section C Life issues 91

C.1	The sanctity of life	92
C.2	Abortion – the facts	94
C.3	Abortion – the religious responses	96
C.4	Abortion – the issues	98
C.5	The cost of going to war	100
C.6	The Just War	102
C.7	The Holy War and pacifism	104
C.8	What are prejudice and discrimination?	106
C.9	Racism	108
C.10	Sexism	110
C.11	Other kinds of prejudice	112
C.12	Religious attitudes to prejudice	114
	Exam questions	116

Section D Planet earth 117

D.1	In the beginning (1)	118
D.2	In the beginning (2)	120
D.3	What can the creation stories teach us?	122
D.4	Science, religion and creation	124
D.5	Human beings and animals	126
D.6	Vegetarianism (1)	128
D.7	Vegetarianism (2)	130
D.8	Vivisection	132
D.9	Hunting and other blood sports	134
D.10	Damaging the planet (1)	136
D.11	Damaging the planet (2)	138
	Exam questions	140

Glossary 141

Understanding the syllabus and this book

This book has been written specifically for the AQA Religious Studies Specification B Module 2 course – 'Key Beliefs, Ultimate Questions and Life Issues'. It will also be very useful for the same topics taught elsewhere – such as AQA Specification A, Options 2A and 2B and Specification B Units 1 and 3. Teachers will also find it very useful for teaching both long and short courses offered by other Examination Boards.

This book has been carefully designed to meet the needs of all students and abilities. It is written in a language that makes it accessible to all by a very experienced and successful author of Religious Studies texts at all levels. The book is arranged in a double-page format with each spread beginning with a 'Key Question' that takes the student to the heart of the topic. The text itself is broken down into easily-digestible chunks which are often bullet-pointed to aid memorising. The technical words in each spread are very important and these are listed under 'Key Words' and a definition of each is found in the Glossary. At least two questions are included in each spread with a 'To Talk About' found in most spreads. There are also 'Exam Tips' dotted throughout the book. A very important feature of each spread is the extract(s) from the holy books and other relevant sources. Each unit finishes with 'Exam Questions'.

The book is organised into four sections following the syllabus. Section A provides an introduction to the basic beliefs of Buddhism, Christianity, Hinduism, Islam, Judaism and Sikhism followed by the principles of Christian morality. Section B focuses on questions of meaning: evidence for and against belief in God; the questions raised by the presence of suffering in the world; and questions surrounding life after death. Section C considers religious questions arising from the life issues of abortion, war and prejudice. Section D invites candidates to explore the religious dimensions of life on earth, both animal and human.

The syllabus allows students to study just one, or up to three, of the six religions. Candidates may only answer a question on one religion in Section A, but in Sections B, C and D they may use two religions in any one answer. On the paper as a whole, candidates may use their knowledge and understanding of up to three religions.

Two other comments about the exam paper:

- There are 'stimulus' questions in questions 8–13 where either an extract from a newspaper or a photo is used to help the student focus their mind on the issue under discussion. Any relevant information provided should be used in the student's answer.
- In the course, students will be expected to show an ability to:
  - remember, select, organise and demonstrate relevant knowledge
  - describe and explain the relevance of religious teachings to the subject
  - evaluate religious and moral responses to the different issues, using both the evidence and also argument.

SECTION A
KEY BELIEFS

In this section you will find out about:

A.1–2	The origins and holy books of Buddhism
A.3–4	The key beliefs of Buddhism
A.5	How Buddhists show their devotion to the teachings of the Buddha
A.6	The origins of Christianity and the importance of the Bible
A.7–8	The key beliefs of Christianity
A.9	How Christians worship
A.10	The service of Holy Communion
A.11	The origins and holy books of Hinduism
A.12–13	The key beliefs of Hinduism
A.14	How Hindus worship
A.15	The origins of Islam and the importance of the Qur'an
A.16–17	The key beliefs of Islam
A.18	The origins of Judaism and the importance of the Torah
A.19–20	The key beliefs of Judaism
A.21–22	The origins of Sikhism and the importance of the Guru Granth Sahib
A.23	The key beliefs of Sikhism
A.24	How Sikhs worship
A.25	How Christians make moral decisions
A.26	The different kinds of love
A.27	Christian love and forgiveness
A.28	Jesus and forgiveness

A.1 The origins of Buddhism (1)

KEY QUESTION
What were the four 'sights' that had such a great impact on Siddattha Gotama?

Siddattha Gotama, who was later called the **Buddha**, was the founder of Buddhism. The son of a rajah (king), he was born about 560 BCE and died at the age of 80. He lived in north-east India at a time when this area was one of the world's greatest intellectual and spiritual centres.

The birth of Siddattha Gotama

There are many legends about the birth of Siddattha Gotama. One legend is that Maya, his mother, dreamed that a white elephant entered her womb and, 10 months later, she gave birth to a child on the day of the full moon in May. The earth trembled and supernatural beings were present at his birth. His mother died four days later because, as the legend says, she who has borne the Buddha cannot serve any other purpose. The baby was given two names:

- Siddattha – meaning 'he who has reached his goal', looking forward to the time when he would be enlightened.
- Gotama – after a famous teacher from whom he was descended.

The young prince was brought up by his aunt in the greatest luxury. She made sure of this because, at his naming ceremony, a wise man had said he would either become a ruler or a wandering holy man. To make sure he became a ruler, his father prevented him from leaving the palace to keep him from seeing all that is unpleasant in life.

The four sights

The young prince married a girl called Gopa (or Yashodara) when he was 19 years old. According to legend, she was outstanding for her beauty, modesty and breeding yet, when she had a son, her husband called him Rahula (chain). In the middle of all his luxury, Siddattha Gotama felt as if he was weighed down by chains.

He escaped from the palace and, during this time, he had four experiences which confronted him with the harsh realities of life outside the palace. He saw the very suffering that his father had tried to shield him from. He saw:

- a frail old man. Until now, no one had told him that people grow old. He could now see for himself that old age destroys memory, beauty and strength.
- an invalid, wracked with pain. He was shocked to see such pain and suffering and 'trembled like the reflection of the moon on rippling water'.
- mourners weeping in a funeral procession. He was deeply concerned by the pain and anguish brought on by death. He did not know that all life ended in death.

An encounter with a Hindu holy man, like the one here, taught Siddattha Gotama that true spiritual contentment was possible.

- a wandering holy man who was deeply contented with his life carrying an alms bowl and living off the gifts of others. He suddenly saw that all of life's pleasures and treasures were worthless. What he now longed for was true 'knowledge'.

Siddattha Gotama left his palace and family in the middle of the night and stole away to look for spiritual enlightenment and knowledge.

EXTRACT A

"*I was spoiled, very spoiled. I anointed myself with only Benares sandalwood and dressed only in Benares cloth. Day and night a white sunshade was held over me. I had a palace for the winter, one for the summer and one for the rainy season. In the four months of the rainy season I did not leave the palace at all and I was surrounded by female musicians.*"

[Siddattha Gotama describing his early life]

EXAM TIPS

You will find many technical words used in this book. Each religion has its own 'vocabulary'. It is most important that you learn the meaning of many of them. You will gain marks by using these words correctly. Learn the meaning of the most important words as you go along.

KEY WORD

Buddha

Work

1. What was thought to be unusual about the birth of Siddattha Gotama?
2. What was important about the name that Siddattha Gotama gave to his son?
3. What were the four sights that Siddattha Gotama saw and what was the significance of each of them for the young prince?

A.2 The origins of Buddhism (2)

Buddhists believe that just by looking at a rupa of the Buddha they are given much of his contentment.

KEY QUESTION How did Siddattha Gotama find enlightenment?

After Siddattha Gotama left home, he began searching for spiritual knowledge, as many Hindu holy men were doing at the time. He tried constant yoga exercises but they did not give him the spiritual knowledge and insight he was seeking. For six years he lived in extreme poverty and self-denial with five companions, but he was still dissatisfied. Legend says that he lived on a single grain of rice a day for this time! In desperation he sat beneath a bodhi tree and started to meditate.

The enlightenment of Siddattha Gotama

During the next three nights, Gotama went through three stages of spiritual enlightenment and resisted the temptations of Mara, the Evil One, who tried to persuade him to enter **nibbana** (paradise) at once. By the end of this time, Gotama saw the whole truth of human existence:

- On the first night he saw his previous lives pass before him. He realised that, when they die, everyone leaves their present body behind and moves on to another. He decided that: "Surely this world is unprotected and helpless, and like a wheel it goes round and round."
- On the second night he saw with supernatural insight the cycle of birth, death and rebirth and recognised the law – the law of karma – that governs it. He saw that the death and rebirth of all living things depend on whether they have done good or bad things in their present life. The threat of death is always present and creatures can never find a resting place.
- On the third night he came to understand the **Four Noble Truths** – the knowledge of suffering, the source of suffering, the removal of suffering and the way to remove the suffering. These were to become the basis of his teaching. He saw that over and over again all living creatures are born, age, pass on to a new life and are reborn. The truth was born in Gotama's mind that people do not know how to escape from this cycle and that is where they need help.

After Gotama's enlightenment, when he became the Buddha (the Enlightened One), he was asked three times by the high God, **Brahma**, to stay behind on earth and help others towards enlightenment by teaching them these truths. This the Buddha did.

After enlightenment

The Buddha preached his first sermon at Benares and his five former companions became his first disciples. Soon this number grew. People were greatly impressed by the serene calm of the preacher. The Buddha sent his disciples out to spread his new teaching. The Buddha himself travelled around India for 44 years living as a beggar-monk. At the age of 80, however, he was taken ill during a meal and died in the town of Kushinagara. Many legends surround his death – they describe his joyful entry into nibbana and the terrible earthquake that shook the land to show the significance of his cremation. Buddhists do not believe that the Buddha was a god – he was a very enlightened human being.

The Tipitaka

The Tipitaka (The Three Baskets) is a vast collection of sacred writings. If you can imagine builders working together and passing baskets of material from one to another, you can probably work out why they are called The Three Baskets. The material was handed down from one generation to another by word of mouth. Eventually, in the 1st century BCE, monks wrote the scriptures on long pieces of palm leaves and arranged them as three separate collections:

1. **The Vinaya Pitaka** – containing the rules for the male and female monastic communities, the **Sangha**. It lists the eight possessions that each monk is allowed to have – an alms bowl, a needle, a razor, a toothpick, a belt and three robes.
2. **The Sutta Pitaka** – the word 'sutta' means 'thread' and this book contains the 'threads' of the teachings of the Buddha – most notably the Four Noble Truths and the Eightfold Path.
3. **The Abhidharmma Pitaka** – the 'higher teachings' began by the Buddha.

The writings of the Tipitaka are chanted as a part of Buddhist devotion. As they are absorbed by each person, so they become a part of the way that they live.

Work

1. Where did Siddattha Gotama try to find the knowledge he was seeking before he was enlightened?
2. Describe the *three* stages that Siddattha Gotama took to enlightenment.
3. What are The Three Baskets and why are they so called?

Key Words

Brahma – Buddha – Eightfold Path – Four Noble Truths – Karma – Nibbana – Sangha

To Talk About

Why do you think that monks in most religions give up almost all of their worldly goods in their search for spiritual truth?

A.3 Key Buddhist teachings (1)

KEY QUESTION What are the Three Universal Truths, the Three Refuges and the Four Noble Truths?

Buddhism does not start with the assumption that God exists, as other religions do. For Buddhists, religion is a way of living in this present life until the highest good has been reached. The Buddha's teachings (**dharma**) work because they offer answers to life's most difficult questions.

The Three Universal Truths

The **Three Universal Truths** are the starting point for the Buddha's teaching.

Truth 1: **Anicca** – everything changes. Everything is impermanent. Nothing, not even mountains, last for ever.

Truth 2: **Anatta** – people are always changing. As soon as a person is born they head towards death. Life is like an ever-rolling wheel with four segments – birth, growth, decay and death. As the wheel turns, so rebirth follows rebirth. From the moment they are born, people begin to change in the five different aspects of their personality – their consciousness, feelings, thoughts, sight or perception and physical body. Nothing stays the same, everything is in flux.

Truth 3: **Dukkha** – suffering. Ordinary life inevitably involves some form of suffering – suffering through illness, accident, old age or death.

The Three Refuges (Jewels)

Buddhists always begin their devotion by reciting aloud the **Three Refuges**:

1 "I go to the Buddha for my refuge." Buddhism has grown out of the teachings of the Buddha and it is there that each Buddhist finds his or her greatest authority. It is impossible to move towards enlightenment without following the teachings of the Buddha.
2 "I go to the teaching (dharma) for my refuge." The dharma is the Buddhist name for the teaching of the holy books. The word itself means 'universal truth', a truth that needs to be responded to and lived out in daily life. That is what a Buddhist tries to do.
3 "I go to the sangha for refuge." The sangha is the entire Buddhist community – the monastic community and the membership of the **vihara**.

TO TALK ABOUT

It is the teaching of Buddhism that 'desire leads to pain'. Do you believe that this is true? Give reasons for your answer, showing that you have considered more than one point of view. Also remember that there are many different ways of understanding pain, and that all pain may not be bad.

Monks are those Buddhists who have decided to set off on a serious quest for enlightenment by following the Middle Way.

The Four Noble Truths

The Buddha taught that all life involves suffering. To find the answer to the problem of suffering a person must accept four 'truths' about themselves and life itself:

Noble Truth 1: Dukkha – This is the truth that life itself is unsatisfactory and so involves suffering. Every life has something wrong with it and this will be true until enlightenment has been reached. The three 'poisons' (ignorance, greed and hatred) increase the amount of suffering for each of us.

Noble Truth 2: Samudaya – Life is full of dukkha because we crave pleasure, power, wealth and our own opinions. People are naturally selfish and greedy. These cravings give rise to quarrels and wars between people and nations.

Noble Truth 3: Nirodha – This is the Buddha's cure for suffering. It involves overcoming selfishness and so releasing ourselves from its cravings. Suffering disappears when you stop wanting things. To do this you must give up believing that everything is permanent and accept that everything is passing and imperfect. If a person continues to live on a worldly level they will be slaves to greed, hatred, sloth, restlessness and doubt.

Noble Truth 4: Magga – This is the Middle Way of the Eightfold Path which is designed to lift a person from the worldly to the spiritual plane of life.
We will look at the Middle Way in Topic A.4.

Key Words

Anicca – Anatta – Buddha – Dharma – Dukkha – Four Noble Truths – Middle Way – Nirodha – Sangha – Three Refuges – Three Universal Truths – Vihara

Work

1. What are the Three Universal Truths or Marks of Existence in Buddhism?
2. What are the Three Refuges or Jewels of Buddhism?
3. Explain the Four Noble Truths of Buddhism?

A.4 Key Buddhist teachings (2)

KEY QUESTION What do Buddhists understand by the Eightfold Path?

The last of the Four Noble Truths taught that there was a **Middle Way** which, if followed, provided the answer to the problem of suffering. It is called the 'Middle Way' because it lies between the life of total self-denial that the Buddha had tried and the way of total pleasure and self-indulgence in which he had been brought up. Instead, the Buddha wanted a way that everyone could follow which did not take them to either of these two extremes. It is called the **Eightfold Path**.

The Eightfold Path

By following the noble Eightfold Path, Buddhists believe that they have found the way to end suffering in their own lives. This is not a path in the sense that each step needs to be taken after the previous one. They all need to be followed at the same time. The steps are:

Step 1: Right viewpoint. Buddhists must accept the teachings of the Buddha in the Four Noble Truths which give them a right understanding of life. They need a vision of what they might become – then they will see things as they really are.

Step 2: Right attitude. People need to be determined to succeed in their journey and to have positive thoughts towards themselves and others.

Steps 1 and 2 show that they are in the right frame of mind to begin the journey.

Step 3: Right speech. The language that people use matters. Unwholesome words are harsh and false – wholesome words are true and helpful. They should not hurt other people by what they say.

Step 4: Right behaviour. They must obey the teaching of the **Five Moral Precepts** of Buddhism (see Extract A). The call is to live an unselfish, charitable life, helping those in need.

> **EXTRACT A**
> "I undertake to abstain from taking life [killing]; taking what is not freely given [stealing]; the misuse of the senses [misusing sex]; wrong speech [lying]; taking drugs and alcohol which cloud the mind."
> [The Five Moral Precepts of Buddhism]

Step 5: Right livelihood. Buddhists must choose their job carefully for the more it helps others the more it will raise them to the spiritual plane. Butchers, for example, are frowned upon because their livelihood leads them to destroy life. If people change their environment frequently, then this will change their level of consciousness. For example, a mountain holiday will enlarge their vision of the greatness of creation.

Steps 3, 4 and 5 show a Buddhist how they should behave once they have decided to undertake the journey towards enlightenment.

Buddhists believe that drinking alcohol clouds the mind and so stands in the way of spiritual enlightenment.

Step 6: Right effort. The mind needs to be trained to avoid those things that are unhelpful and evil. There are four different meditations, called the Four Sublime States, which can be used to bring this about. These meditations, however, will only help someone to live happily in this world. They will not give them complete freedom or insight into the truth. To find this, another step must be taken.

Step 7: Right mindfulness. This step requires a Buddhist to eliminate all unwholesome or selfish thoughts from their mind. To do this, they must stand outside themselves and see themselves as they really are – only then can they cope with all their cravings. They can only do this through meditation.

Step 8: Right concentration. Now meditation reaches its peak and they will become 'absorbed' – just as soap powder is absorbed in water. They will find bliss and ecstasy. They will discard all desires and worried thoughts. They will see everything in its right light and realise that true satisfaction can never be reached through earthly things. They will have reached the state of bliss called nibbana – the 'going out' or 'cooling off' of a flame (see Extract B). A person can reach the state of nibbana in this life and continue in it when their human self dies. When they reach nibbana they are free from the cycle of birth, death and rebirth.

EXTRACT B
"*If you ask, 'How is Nirvana [nibbana] to be known?' it is by freedom from distress and danger, by confidence, by peace, by happiness, by delicacy, by purity, by freshness.*"

[Milanda Panha]

TO TALK ABOUT
If you could control your speech, your behaviour and your cravings/desires, do you think that you would be a happier and better person?

KEY WORDS
Buddha – Eightfold Path – Five Moral Precepts – Four Noble Truths – Middle Way – Nibbana

Work

1. What is the Middle Way and why is it so called?
2. What do Buddhists mean when they talk about nibbana?

A.5 Buddhist devotion

KEY QUESTION How do Buddhists show their devotion to the Buddha and his teachings?

Buddhists do not believe in God. In their devotions they cannot offer up worship in the sense that members of other religions do. Instead, their devotion is a part of their own spiritual journey towards enlightenment. During this journey, great respect is paid to the Buddha and his teachings.

There is no special day in Buddhism for offering devotion at home or in the vihara, although the days before the moon is new, full or at half-moon are particularly important to Buddhists. Many Buddhists believe that the Buddha was born, gained enlightenment and died when there was a full moon in the heavens.

Devotion in the home and at the shrine

Many Buddhists have a shrine in their own home but, those who do not, visit the shrine in the vihara. This contains an image or statue of the Buddha, called a rupa, as well as many other important symbols such as:

- flowers to show the impermanence of life, as they only bloom for a short while before dying – just like human beings.
- candles with their light symbolising the enlightenment which every Buddhist is seeking.
- incense with its smell filling the house to show the sweetness of the Buddha's message.

Buddhists recite the Three Refuges (Jewels) in front of the shrine and also the Five Moral Precepts. They also meditate to help them focus their mind, during which they may chant the **mantra** OM MANI PADME HUM ('the jewel of the lotus brings wisdom').

Flags, wheels, beads and meditation

As Buddhists do not believe in a personal god, so they do not pray in the usual sense. When Buddhists pray, they feel that they are releasing 'the Buddha within'. This means that their devotion to the Buddha and his teaching sets their true nature within themselves free. To some Buddhists this is a form of meditation, while to others it is a display of their devotion to the Buddha's teachings.

In some Buddhist countries, flags fly carrying the words of a mantra. Buddhists believe that, when the wind blows, the blessing of the mantra is released and the energy contained in the mantra is released on the wind. Similarly, in Tibet and elsewhere, mantras are tucked into prayer wheels which are then spun so that the positive energy they contain is released.

EXTRACT A
"*Just touching and turning a prayer wheel brings incredible purification and accumulates unbelievable merit.*" [Lama Zopa Rinpoche, an important Buddhist teacher]

Acts of Buddhist worship are designed to show devotion to the teaching of the Buddha, as well as to further the journey towards enlightenment.

Many Buddhists use **mala beads** to help them to meditate. There are 108 beads on a string and these help worshippers to release interfering thoughts by focusing the mind on an object. In Tibet, bells are seen as objects of wisdom and some Buddhists use them in their meditating. Meditation involves emptying the mind of all unwholesome thoughts, worries and lusts by cultivating thoughts which are wholesome and encourage joy and peace of mind. As meditation removes stress, so it benefits the body, physically and mentally.

There are different forms of meditation, two of which are:

- samatha meditation. This was a form practised by the Buddha and so it is used by his followers today. It concentrates on controlling the breathing and this enables the mind to settle down at rest. As the air moves smoothly through the body, so do peace and tranquillity.
- vipassana or insight meditation. When samatha meditation has calmed the mind then vipassana meditation, with its detached observation, allows a person to examine things, emotions and other people clearly. For example, if you wonder why you are so often angry, it may help to stand outside of yourself so that you can watch your anger subsiding. This has an obvious link with the seventh step on the Eightfold Path – right mindfulness.

TO TALK ABOUT

Can you see any value in meditation as a spiritual exercise? Why do you think so many people are learning to meditate these days?

KEY WORDS

Buddha – Eightfold Path – Five Moral Precepts – Mala beads – Mantra – Three Refuges – Vihara

Work

1. What are prayer wheels and why are they found in many Buddhist temples?
2. Why are flowers, candles and incense found in many Buddhist homes and temples?
3. What do Buddhists understand by prayer?
4. Describe *two* forms of Buddhist meditation.

A.6 The origins of Christianity

KEY QUESTION What do we know about the life and teaching of Jesus of Nazareth?

The Christian religion began with **Jesus** of Nazareth. The only useful record that we have of his life, teaching and death is found in the four **Gospels** of the New Testament. The first of these, Mark's Gospel, was not written until about 40 years after Jesus' death while the last, John's Gospel, was not written for a further 35 years. For a long time, therefore, most of the information about Jesus was passed around and kept alive by 'word of mouth'.

The birth and work of Jesus

The country of Palestine was under Roman occupation when an unmarried Jewish couple, Joseph and Mary, received the news from an angel that they were going to be the parents of God's Son. Many Christians believe that the conception of Jesus itself was a miracle. Two of the Gospels tell us that Jesus was conceived miraculously by the **Holy Spirit** in the womb of Mary. This is called the **Virgin birth**.

We are told that, after Jesus was baptised by John the Baptist in the River Jordan at the age of 30, Jesus became a public figure for just three years. He began by choosing 12 disciples with whom he shared the rest of his life. Jesus spent most of this time teaching his disciples about the Kingdom of God on earth or travelling throughout Palestine, helping and healing those in need. During this time, Jesus performed a number of miracles. These miracles fall into three groups:

1. Miracles of physical healing – e.g. healing a man with leprosy (Matthew 8.2–3) and a paralysed man (Mark 2.1–12).
2. Miracles which displayed his power over the destructive forces of nature – e.g. calming a storm (Matthew 8.23–27) and walking on water (John 6.19).
3. Miracles in which people were brought back to life from the dead – e.g. raising Jairus' daughter (Mark 5.22–42), a widow's son (Luke 7.11–15) and Lazarus (John 11.38–44).

The teaching of Jesus

The main theme of the teaching of Jesus was the coming of God's kingdom on earth (see Extract A). To everyone's amazement, he taught that the religious leaders would not be the first to enter this kingdom – if they entered it at all! In front of them would be social outcasts such as the tax collectors, the poor and prostitutes. He taught largely in the form of **parables**, which were everyday stories that carried a religious or moral meaning.

> **EXTRACT A**
> "The right time has come… and the Kingdom of God is near! Turn away from your sins and believe the Good News!"
>
> [Mark 1.15]

The birth of Jesus is celebrated by Christians throughout the world at the festival of Christmas.

Jesus was a Jew and much of his teaching brought him into conflict with the Jewish leaders of the time – especially since he directed much of it against them! The two most important religious groups were the Pharisees and the Sadducees and they came together to plot against Jesus. The extent to which they were responsible for securing the death of Jesus, however, is hotly disputed since the main blame for this falls squarely on the Romans – they alone could sentence a person to death and carry that sentence out in Palestine.

Key Words

Gospel – Holy Spirit – Jesus – New Testament – Parable – Virgin birth

To Talk About

The first Gospel was not written down until about 40 years after the death of Jesus. Do you think that this makes it unreliable?

Work

1. a) What do you think a miracle is? Write a definition in your folder.
    b) Do you think that miracles can, and do, happen? Explain your answer.
    c) How important do you think miracles were in the ministry of Jesus?
    d) What do you think the miracles of Jesus tell us about him?

2. a) What is meant by the Virgin birth?
    b) Whether or not Jesus was born to a virgin, the belief does make an important point about Jesus. What is it?

A.7 Key Christian beliefs (1)

KEY QUESTION What do Christians understand by the Trinity?

The Christian faith is built upon the basic belief that there is only one God. This is a belief called monotheism, which Christianity shares with the religious faith out of which it grew – Judaism. Christianity, however, goes further than Judaism when it teaches that God reveals Himself to the world in three different forms – as God the Father, God the Son and God the Holy Spirit. The relationship between the three different members of the Godhead is what Christians mean when they speak of the **Trinity**.

God the Father

There are two important 'truths' about God in the **Bible**. They are:

1. God is the Creator of everything that exists. The Bible begins with the story of God making the universe, the heavens and the earth. God not only started off this process but He continues it today – as old life dies so new life is created.
2. God is continually interested in the life that He has created – just as parents show a continual interest in the welfare of their children. Jesus expressed this when he spoke of God caring for every sparrow and numbering the hairs on every human head (Matthew 10.29–31).

The favourite title of Jesus for God was 'Father' and he encouraged his followers to begin their prayers by addressing God in the same way (Matthew 6.9).

God the Son

Although everyone is God's son or daughter since they are made in the 'image of God', the Bible makes it clear that Jesus was uniquely the Son of God. The **Incarnation** (the birth of God in human flesh) is at the heart of Christianity. Paul provided a summary of the life of Jesus which explains what early Christians believed about the Incarnation of Jesus (see Extract A).

> **EXTRACT A**
> "He always had the nature of God but he did not think that by force he should remain equal with God. Instead of this, of his own free will he gave up all that he had, and took the nature of a servant. He became like a human being and appeared in human likeness. He was humble and walked the path of obedience all the way to death – his death on the cross."
>
> [Philippians 2.6–8]

You will find out more about Christian beliefs about Jesus in Topic A.8.

The Holy Spirit, the third member of the Christian Trinity, is most frequently portrayed as a dove to show that he is the bringer of God's peace.

God the Holy Spirit

Before he left the earth, Jesus promised his disciples that he would send them a 'Comforter' who would constantly be with them. Christians believe that this happened on the day of **Pentecost** when the Holy Spirit was sent and the **Church** was born (Acts 2). The Church would soon pass through a time of great persecution and it was promised that the Holy Spirit would be an 'Advocate'. The Holy Spirit would help Christians to defend their faith when they appeared before emperors and tribunals by telling them what to say. Christians today believe that the Holy Spirit helps them in a similar way to speak about their faith.

To sum up

The revelation of the Trinity was expressed in the baptismal faith and worship of the early Church. It became part of the Church's worship, preaching and teaching. The **Nicene** and the **Apostles' Creeds** tried to express it in the language of the time, although they did not actually use the word 'Trinity'. They were very careful to avoid all suggestion that the Christian Church believed in three Gods. There are not three Gods – only God in three persons. It works like this:

- God the Father has shown Himself as the Creator who sent Jesus into the world.
- Jesus showed everyone what God was like and died to save the world.
- God continues to make Himself known in the world today through the Holy Spirit.

Key Words

Apostles' Creed – Bible – Church – Holy Spirit – Incarnation – Jesus – Nicene Creed – Paul – Pentecost – Trinity

Work

1. Write down *three* things that Christians believe about God the Father.
2. Write down *three* things that Christians believe about the Holy Spirit.

Exam tips

When writing an answer, it is very important to select the key points you wish to make. Read each question carefully and identify the key points before you put pen to paper.

A.8 Key Christian beliefs (2)

> **KEY QUESTION** What do Christians believe about Jesus, salvation and eternal life?

Christian beliefs about Jesus are the backbone of the Church's worship – its prayers, hymns and Bible readings. Behind these beliefs lies a very long history during which Christians have reflected on, and disagreed about, what it means to believe in Jesus as 'God in human flesh'.

Christians believe that the death of Jesus on the cross was part of God's plan for the salvation of the human race.

Jesus of Nazareth

Christians believe that:

- Jesus was God in human form (see Extract A). He was conceived in Mary's womb by the Holy Spirit and was God's only Son. When Jesus was baptised by John the Baptist in the River Jordan at the beginning of his public ministry, Jesus heard God's voice from heaven telling him: "You are my own dear Son. I am pleased with you." (Mark 1.11)
- Jesus died at the hands of Pontius Pilate, the Roman procurator, around 29 CE. The Bible makes it clear that the death of Jesus was part of God's plan to save the world. Paul described this divine plan as bringing the human race back into a close relationship with God – the **Atonement** ('making-at-one'). Christians remember the death of Jesus each year on **Good Friday** at the end of **Holy Week**.
- Jesus was brought back to life by God three days after he was crucified. The **Resurrection** stands at the very heart of the Christian faith. Christians celebrate the Resurrection of Jesus on **Easter Sunday**. See Extract A for a summary of early Christian belief about Jesus.

> **EXTRACT A**
> "I believe in God, the Father the almighty, creator of heaven and earth. I believe in Jesus Christ, his only Son, our Lord, who was conceived by the Holy Spirit, born of the Virgin Mary, suffered under Pontius Pilate, was crucified, died and was buried; he descended to the dead. On the third day he rose again; he ascended into heaven; he is seated at the right hand of the Father, and will come again to judge the living and the dead..."
>
> [The Apostles' Creed]

20

Salvation and eternal life

The Resurrection of Jesus is believed by Christians to show that Jesus was God's Son and that there is eternal life for all who believe in him. The resurrection is the guarantee that all Christians will rise from the dead at the end of time. Two incidents in the life of Jesus are relevant here:

- The rich young ruler (Luke 18.18–30). A rich young ruler asked Jesus how he could receive eternal life. He said that he had kept all of God's commandments, so Jesus told him to sell everything that he had and give the proceeds to the poor. The man was not able to do this.
- Zacchaeus (Luke 19.1–10). Zacchaeus was a much hated tax collector but Jesus visited him. Zacchaeus told Jesus that he would give half of his belongings to the poor and pay back four times the amount he had taken falsely. Jesus told him that salvation had now come to his house.

> **EXTRACT B**
> "...you remember that ever since you were a child, you have known the Holy Scriptures, which are able to give you the wisdom that leads to salvation through faith in Christ Jesus. All Scripture is inspired by God and is useful for teaching the truth, rebuking error, correcting faults, and giving instruction for right living..."
> [2 Timothy 3.15–16]

The Bible

The Bible is unique because it contains books which are sacred to the followers of two religions:

- The **Old Testament** (Jews and Christians). The books of the Old Testament were written over a period of about 2,000 years and include laws, prophecies, history, poetry, myths, songs and stories. These tell the story of the Jewish people from the time of **Abraham**, around 2000 BCE, through to the years preceding the occupation of the Jewish homeland by the Romans in 63 BCE. Most of the early followers of Jesus were Jews and they would have been brought up to love their scriptures. Extract B is Paul's summary of the Jewish scriptures.
- The **New Testament** (Christians). The books of the New Testament tell the story of Jesus and the early Church. The earliest books are the letters written by the early Church leaders such as **Peter**, **Paul** and John. The four Gospels – Matthew, Mark, Luke and John – are our only record of the birth, life, teachings, death and Resurrection of Jesus.

KEY WORDS

Abraham – Atonement – Bible – Church – Easter Sunday – Good Friday – Gospel – Holy Spirit – Holy Week – Jesus – New Testament – Old Testament – Paul – Peter – Resurrection

Work

1. What do Christians mean by the Atonement?
2. Why do Christians believe that the Resurrection of Jesus was so important?
3. What do the incidents of the rich young ruler and Zacchaeus have to say about salvation and eternal life?
4. Write *four* sentences about the Bible.

A.9 Christian worship

KEY QUESTION What are the two different styles of Christian worship?

The word 'worship' means 'worth-ship' and Christians want to make their worship worthy of God. The hymns, the prayers, the Bible readings and the sermon that make up an act of Christian worship are all designed to express the honour that is due to God alone. Broadly speaking, this worship can be divided into two distinct styles.

The liturgical style of worship

This style of worship is typical of **Anglican**, **Roman Catholic** and **Orthodox** churches. It follows a set pattern, called the **liturgy**, which is set down in a prayer book. The prayer book that Roman Catholics use is called the **Missal**, while the oldest Anglican prayer book is the **Book of Common Prayer**. More recent Anglican prayer books have been the Alternative Service Book and Common Worship. In the Orthodox Church the order of service is called the **Divine Liturgy**.

Many people prefer a liturgical and more structured style of worship because they:

- know that, wherever they are worshipping, the service will be familiar to them.
- have been brought up to worship in this way and they feel comfortable with it.
- find the service easy to follow because they have it in front of them.
- want an emphasis on the **sacraments** in their worship, especially Holy Communion, and a liturgical style of worship gives this to them.

TO TALK ABOUT

Why do you think that taking part in acts of worship is very important to many people? Is it important to you? Why?

This service, being held in a Catholic church, is an example of the liturgical style of worship.

This service, being held in a Baptist church, is an example of a non-liturgical style of worship.

The non-liturgical style of worship

The approach of most **Protestant churches** towards worship is different. Non-liturgical services are common in the **Baptist** and Pentecostal denominations. Many people prefer them because they believe that their services are open to the leading of the Holy Spirit. The emphasis is upon singing, prayers that follow no set pattern (called 'extempore' prayers), readings from the Bible and the sermon. Services often also include personal testimonies by worshippers, describing how God has worked in their lives.

Many people prefer non-liturgical services because:

- every service is different and less predictable than liturgical services.
- people feel free to express their feelings by clapping, dancing, joining in the prayers, waving their arms in the air, etc.
- people do not become over-familiar with the services. There is always something unexpected happening.

Quaker worship is different to both of these forms of worship. Quakerism goes back to the 17th century and is largely based upon silence as people wait to hear 'the voice within' speaking to them. The silence is only broken if someone feels prompted to share what the Holy Spirit has said to them with others.

Key Words

Anglican Church – Baptist Church – Bible – Book of Common Prayer – Divine Liturgy – Holy Communion – Holy Spirit – Liturgy – Missal – Orthodox Church – Protestant Church – Quaker – Roman Catholic Church – Sacrament

Work

1. What does worship mean to a Christian?
2. a) What is meant by liturgical worship?
   b) Why do many Christians prefer a liturgical form of worship?
3. a) What is meant by non-liturgical worship?
   b) Why do many Christians prefer to take part in non-liturgical acts of worship?

23

A.10 Holy Communion

KEY QUESTION What is the significance of the service of Holy Communion to Christians?

For most Christians, the service of **Holy Communion**, or the **Eucharist**, is their most important act of worship. Holy Communion means 'holy sharing' and is the service in which believers share bread and wine with each other – and with God. They do this to share spiritually in the death of Jesus.

For most Christians, the service of Holy Communion is their most important act of worship.

In the beginning

It is the clear link between Holy Communion and the life of Jesus (see Extract A) that gives this sacrament its unique place in the Church's worship. From the day of Pentecost onwards, we are told that the early Christians met together 'to break bread'. They did this because it was what Jesus told them to do (Extract A).

All four Gospels and one of the **Epistles** (1 Corinthians) record what happened when Jesus shared his last meal with his disciples – a meal called the **Last Supper**. We are told that, on the night on which he was betrayed, Jesus took a loaf of bread, broke it, and gave a piece to each of his disciples, saying: "Take and eat it. This is my body." Moments later he took a goblet of wine and passed it around with the words: "Drink it, all of you… this is my blood, which seals God's covenant, my blood poured out for many for the forgiveness of sins." (Matthew 26.26–28.)

These words form the basis of the service of Holy Communion today.

KEY WORDS

Anglican Church – Baptist Church – Breaking of Bread – Divine Liturgy – Epistle – Eucharist – Gospel – Holy Communion – Jesus – Last Supper – Liturgy – Lord's Supper – Mass – Orthodox Church – Paul – Pentecost – Protestant Church – Roman Catholic Church – Sacrament – Transubstantiation

EXTRACT A

"*Then he took a piece of bread, gave thanks to God, broke it, and gave it to them, saying, 'This is my body which is given for you. Do this in memory of me.' In the same way, he gave them the cup after the supper, saying, 'This cup is God's new covenant sealed with my blood, which is poured out for you.*"

[Luke 22.19–20]

One service – different names

The different Christian churches have their own names for this service:

- In the Anglican Church it is called Holy Communion or the Eucharist ('thanksgiving').
- In the Roman Catholic Church it is called the **Mass**, probably from the final words of the old Latin service – 'Ita Missa Est' ('Go, it is finished').
- In the Orthodox Church it is called the Divine Liturgy. The 'liturgy' is the traditional order of service and the service used in the Divine Liturgy goes back, unchanged, to the 4th century.
- Nonconformists, such as Baptists and Pentecostalists, call it the **Breaking of Bread** or the **Lord's Supper**. The Gospels tell us that Jesus 'broke bread' (shared a meal) with his disciples at the Last Supper while the phrase 'the Lord's Supper' is taken from the writings of Paul.

The meaning of Holy Communion

There is a real difference between the way that Roman Catholics or Orthodox Christians and Protestants understand Holy Communion. This difference has been at the heart of many bitter disputes between them in the past. The difference revolves around what is believed to happen to the bread and the wine during the service:

- The Roman Catholic and Orthodox Churches believe that Christ is really 'present' in the bread and wine. The bread and wine become the actual body and blood of Jesus as they are offered up to God as a sacrifice by the priest. This belief is called **transubstantiation**.
- Most Anglican and other Protestant churches believe that the service is largely one of remembrance by which those who eat the bread and drink the wine receive a spiritual blessing. Throughout the service the elements remain what they are – bread and wine.

TO TALK ABOUT

Why do you think that, from the beginning, the Christian Church felt it necessary to celebrate the death of Jesus regularly?

Work

1. a) What do the bread and wine at the service of Holy Communion symbolise?
   b) Give *two* other names by which the service of Holy Communion is known.
   c) Explain what it is that makes the service of Holy Communion unique among the sacraments.
2. Why is the Eucharist often described by Christians as a service of Holy Communion?

EXAM TIPS

There are many different technical words in this topic. There is no substitute for learning the meaning of many, if not all, of them.

A.11 THE ORIGINS AND HOLY BOOKS OF

KEY QUESTION What are the different Hindu holy books?

It is not easy to pinpoint just how, when and where Hinduism began. Unlike the other major world religions, the teachings of Hinduism cannot be traced back to a single individual. Instead, they are based on the teachings of many religious thinkers who lived at different times. Their teachings are collected together in many different holy books.

The origins of Hinduism

The roots of Hinduism are found in the Indus Valley civilisation which grew up around the banks of the River Indus in about 2000 BCE. The civilisation was very advanced, with large houses and towns and producing a highly glazed form of pottery. Many statues of the Mother Goddess have been unearthed, suggesting a strong emphasis on fertility.

The prosperity of this group began to decline around 1500 BCE as the Aryans moved into India. They built great cities along the River Ganges and intermarried with the Indus people. Their religions soon intermingled. It is out of this mixture that Hinduism grew. By 400 BCE Hinduism had taken on the characteristics it has today. The Aryans provided the Hindus with their earliest scriptures – the **Rig Veda** – and a later important collection of writings – the **Upanishads**.

The holy books of Hinduism

There are many holy books in Hinduism. They are used extensively for personal devotions and acts of worship (**puja**) carried out both at home in front of the family shrine and in the **mandir** (temple). The holy books also play an important role in such ceremonies as the **Sacred Thread** ceremony and marriage. These books fall into two groups:

1 The **shruti** – 'that which is heard'. These are the books which were believed to have been directly received by holy men from God. The shruti contains:

- the **Vedas**. These are the oldest known Hindu books and are written in Sanskrit. There are four groups of Vedas and the most important of these is the Rig Veda. This contains over 1,000 hymns offered in praise of 33 different gods. You can find an extract of the material in the Rig Veda in Extract A.
- the Upanishads. This title means 'sitting near' and contains some of the teachings given by **gurus** (holy men) to their pupils.

EXTRACT A
"What sin we have ever committed against an intimate, O Varuna, against a friend or a companion at any time, a brother, a neighbour, or a stranger, free us from it, O Varuna."

[Rig Veda]

Hinduism

Many Hindu books contain epic stories in which the gods come to earth and live among human beings.

2 **The smriti** – 'that which is remembered'. These books are based on human recollections of God's message. They are later books and considered to be less important but include some of the best-loved holy books of Hinduism. Among the books in this category are:

- epics including the **Mahabharata** and the **Ramayana**. The Mahabharata is the world's longest poem, containing over three million words. This poem includes the **Bhagavad Gita**, which tells of two royal families who fight over who should rule the land. The god **Krishna** disguises himself as a charioteer and tells Arjuna that it is his duty to fight even if some members of his family are killed. The Ramayana contains the story of Prince Rama and his wife, Sita. Sita is kidnapped by the evil demon Ravana but Rama rescues her with the help of the god Hanuman and an army of monkeys. The story illustrates a common theme of Hindu holy books – that good will always triumph over evil in the end.
- the Laws of Manu. This is a book containing instructions that Hindus should follow in their daily lives. It also includes the punishments that should be given to those who commit certain crimes and the rules that priests are expected to follow.

Key Words

Bhagavad Gita – Guru – Krishna – Mahabharata – Mandir – Puja – Ramayana – Rig Veda – Sacred Thread – Shruti – Smriti – Upanishads – Vedas

Work

1. Describe the origins of Hinduism.
2. How do Hindus make use of their holy books?
3. Write *three* sentences about each of the following:
   a) The shruti.
   b) The smriti.

To Talk About

Most Hindu holy books teach that good will always triumph over evil in the end. Do you share this optimism or do you think that it is misplaced?

A.12 Key Hindu beliefs (1)

KEY QUESTION What do Hindus believe about God?

There are thought to be 330 million gods and goddesses in Hinduism, but only **Brahman** is seen as the Ultimate Reality. All of the other gods and goddesses are the human face of Brahman. This means that Hinduism is a monotheistic religion which believes in only one God.

◀ Hindus pray to Ganesha for his help in their everyday lives.

Brahman

Hindus see God in the impersonal, neuter form which they call Brahman as well as in the personalities of all their gods and goddesses. Hindus describe Brahman as the 'ultimate, holy power', the one Spirit God, the supreme soul of the universe. Brahman is present everywhere and is like a powerhouse 'lighting up' all the other gods and goddesses. These gods then reflect or illuminate the greatness of Brahman.

Atman

The presence of Brahman in every human being is called the **atman**. It is usually translated as the 'spirit' or the 'soul'. Just like Brahman, the atman is eternal and is pure spirit. The human body grows old and dies but not the atman, which passes through successive rebirths until, eventually, it is reunited with the Brahman (Extract A).

> **EXTRACT A**
> "Just as a person casts off worn-out garments and puts on others, even so the embodied soul casts off worn-out bodies and takes on others that are new… The self is the same forever: unmanifest, unthinkable, still."
> [The Bhagavad Gita ii 22–25]

The triad of gods

One way in which the Supreme Spirit, Brahman, is revealed is as the **Trimurti**, or triad, of great gods: Brahma (the Creator); **Vishnu** (the preserver); and **Shiva** (the destroyer and re-creator). Of these three, Vishnu and Shiva are the most widely worshipped of all Hindu deities. Vishnu is referred to in the scriptures as the luckiest of the gods, standing for compassion, law and order. He has visited the earth nine times in different forms and these are called **avatars**. Shiva takes on a variety of forms, summed up in his 1,008 names. Many of these names refer to Shiva's control over the natural world – such as the 'Mountain Lord' and the 'Bearer of the Ganges'.

Hindu deities

Although there are millions of manifestations of the gods, Hindu believers usually direct their prayers to a single god or goddess – often one that has been worshipped by previous generations of their family. At special times, however, such as the birth of a new baby, they pray to other gods as well. Among the most popular Hindu deities are:

- Krishna. Krishna was the eighth avatar of Vishnu and also a god in his own right. Usually portrayed as a child or a young man, he often carries a flute. Devotees maintain that Krishna had a happy childhood and so brings them happiness. Many colourful stories about Krishna are told in the Mahabharata and the Puranas.
- **Ganesha**. Ganesha is the god of wisdom, who has the power to help human beings and is known as 'the remover of obstacles'. Before any new undertaking – such as taking an exam or getting married – Hindus present their offerings to Ganesha. Ganesha didn't originally have an elephant's head. His father, the great god Shiva, accidentally beheaded him and, to bring him back to life, cut off the head of a passing elephant and placed it on his son's shoulders.
- **Rama**. The Lord Rama, the seventh avatar of Vishnu, is seen as the perfect son, husband and ruler. These exceptional qualities make him the perfect example for Hindu men to follow.
- **Lakshmi**. One of the most popular of Hindu deities, Lakshmi is the goddess of wealth, beauty and good luck. She is the faithful consort of Vishnu in all his avatars.
- **Kali**. She can have a peaceful nature as Parvati or a fierce and bloodthirsty one as Kali. In her bloodthirsty guise, Kali is shown with a necklace of skulls and a skirt of severed hands.

▲ The god Krishna is one of the most popular of all Hindu gods. He was one of the last avatars of the god Vishnu.

Key Words

Atman – Avatar – Brahma – Brahman – Ganesha – Krishna – Lakshmi – Mahabharata – Rama – Shiva – Trimurti – Vishnu

Work

1. a) What is an avatar?
   b) Describe *two* of the avatars of Vishnu.
2. a) Who is the god of wisdom?
   b) Describe the appearance of this god using the photograph on page 28.

Exam tips

It is very easy to fall into the trap of thinking that Hinduism is a polytheistic religion with millions of gods. Hinduism is a monotheistic religion with the many gods highlighting different aspects of Brahman's personality.

A.13 Key Hindu beliefs (2)

KEY QUESTION What are the four Hindu aims in life?

There are four aims or goals in life for which every Hindu strives. Taken together, they are believed to guarantee spiritual and social harmony.

The four aims of life

The four aims in life for every Hindu are:

1 **Artha** (worldly wealth and success). This is a proper goal to have in life as long as it is pursued without desire, anger and greed. Early Hindus argued that people needed artha if they were to practise religion. Pursuing an occupation to acquire wealth is justified as long as dharma (see aim 3 below) is not violated.

2 **Kama** (pleasure and desire). This, too, is a legitimate goal for a person's life as long as it does not violate dharma. This is the pursuit of pleasurable activities such as sex, play, recreation, the arts and literature. *The Kama Sutra*, written in the 3rd or 4th century, deals at length with giving and receiving sexual pleasure.

3 **Dharma** (virtue, morality). This has two levels – one's own particular set of values and absolute morality, universally valid. When profit and pleasure are pursued for themselves then they lead to chaos in society.

4 **Moksha** (spiritual liberation). This is the ultimate Hindu goal. It is release from the bondage of suffering and rebirth (see samsara on page 31).

You can find the six greatest blessings in life in Extract A.

EXTRACT A
"Health, freedom from debts, living in one's home country, association with good people, a secure income and a safe dwelling are the six great fortunes of men."
[Mahabharata V. 183]

Three important Hindu beliefs

Three beliefs are at the heart of Hinduism:

1 **Ahimsa**. Ahimsa means having respect for the whole of creation and not killing any forms of life. This is why most Hindus are vegetarians. During the struggle of India for independence in the 1940s, the Indians were led by Mahatma Gandhi. Gandhi was a Hindu who taught that all religions should be respected and that the principle of non-violence was a very important spiritual belief. He encouraged his followers to oppose the British by using non-cooperation without any violence. It was a successful struggle. The Hindu commitment to non-violence can also be seen in its attitude to the cow, which is treated as a sacred animal. Because the cow is not killed, there are said to be as many cows in India as human beings – and that is a lot of cows!

As cows are a sacred animal for Hindus, they are never slaughtered for food.

2. **Karma.** Karma is central to the Hindu belief in **reincarnation**. It teaches that a person's actions in this life determine their condition in this life and their rebirth in the next. Every action has its inevitable fruit or consequence. Good deeds result in good karma – good fortune in this life and a good rebirth in the next. Similarly, bad deeds result in bad karma – misfortune in this life and a bad rebirth. It may result in a person being reborn much lower down the social scale or coming back as an animal.

3. **Samsara.** Many Hindus, especially those in the higher castes, believe in the endless cycle of rebirth (samsara). Efforts to bring the cycle to an end are at the heart of many Hindu religious practices. The intention is to break this cycle of rebirth and so achieve moksha (liberation).

Key Words

Ahimsa – Dharma – Karma – Moksha – Reincarnation – Samsara

To Talk About

Reincarnation is one of two great religious ideas about life after death – Sikhs, Buddhists and Hindus believe in reincarnation. If you were to ask a Sikh, a Buddhist or a Hindu why they believe in reincarnation, what do you think they might say?

Work

1. What are the *four* aims of life for each Hindu? Explain each one.
2. What do Hindus mean by 'ahimsa'?
3. What do Hindus mean by 'karma'?
4. What do Hindus mean by 'samsara'?

A.14 Hindu worship

KEY QUESTION How and where do Hindus worship?

Hindus can worship at home or in their local temple. Some Hindus, however, never visit the temple because the main focus of worship for most believers is the home shrine.

Worship in the home

Many Hindu homes have niches in the wall or a small shrine on a table so that offerings can be made by members of the family. The home is used in this way because it is the basic unit in Hindu society and is given the main responsibility for safeguarding Hindu traditions and customs. Within the family, children are brought up to observe the five daily duties of every Hindu:

1. To carry out some yoga and meditation.
2. To show reverence and to offer frequent worship to the family god.
3. To show an unquestioning respect for the elders and ancestors of the family.
4. To extend the hospitality of the family to all those who are needy and to holy men and women.
5. To display a respect and kindness to all living creatures.

Worship (puja) will only be offered at the shrine to one god and it begins by lighting a lamp which has its wick dipped in ghee (melted butter). Incense sticks are also lit and the names of God are repeated along with the daily prayer – the **Gyatri Mantra** (see Extract A).

A reading from one of the holy books takes place in front of a **mandala** – a mystical design intended to help the mind concentrate on God or the self. During this time, the worshipper

EXTRACT A
"Let us meditate on the glorious light of the creator. May he guide our minds and inspire us with understanding."
[The Gyatri Mantra]

sits upright and cross-legged on the floor, breathing deeply to aid concentration. The sacred syllable, **AUM**, is chanted over and over again. A flame is passed from one to another as a symbol of the god.

Worship in the temple

Many Hindus visit the mandir regularly and here worship starts at dawn as the priest greets, washes and dresses the image of the god. People come forward to offer their worship which has three parts:

1. **Havan** (the offering of fire). The sacred fire is kindled on the altar to symbolise the god devouring the offerings. Each person symbolically washes each part of their body.

The most important Hindu worship takes place in the home and not in the temple.

2 **Arti** (the welcoming ceremony). A flat tray, with five candles, is waved in front of the shrine. The candles represent the five elements – fire, earth, water, air and ether. The worshippers pass their hands over the flame and over their head. This allows them to receive God's blessing.
3 **Bhajan** (singing hymns). Bells, triangles and tambourines are played and some people dance. The worshippers then offer their bhakti (devotion) by lighting a candle and saying prayers. As they leave, they are given prashad (sacred food) which has been offered to the god earlier in the day.

Meditation

Yoga is a discipline designed to help the person gain control over their body and mind. It is a way of controlling negative feelings – such as anger, lust and greed – which prevent a person from entering into union with God. Meditation is an important part of Hinduism for many believers. There are many different positions which help a person work their way towards moksha (liberation from all human desires). Sometimes the worshipper chants a mantra and sometimes they focus their mind on an external object to aid their meditation.

TO TALK ABOUT

Hindus spend much time trying to quieten their minds and bodies as a preliminary to worship and prayer.
   a) Why do you think they consider this to be very important?
   b) How do you try to quieten your body and mind?

Work

1. What are the *five* daily duties of every Hindu?
2. What are the *three* parts to public worship?
3. What is meditation and how does a Hindu carry it out?

Key Words

AUM – Gyatri Mantra – Mandala – Mandir – Mantra – Moksha – Puja – Yoga

A.15 The Origins of Islam

KEY QUESTION What are the origins of Islam?

Islam, a word meaning 'surrendering', began with the revelations and teachings given to **Muhammad** ﷺ, the **Prophet**, by **Allah**.

The early life of Muhammad ﷺ

Muhammad ﷺ was born in **Makkah** in 570 CE but never knew his father, who died before he was born. His mother died when he was six years old and the young Muhammad ﷺ was brought up first by his grandfather and then by his uncle, Abu Talib. When he grew up, Muhammad ﷺ became a camel-driver and then a trader. Because of his honesty in business he became known as 'Al-Amin' (the 'trustworthy one'). He worked for **Khadijah**, a rich widow, and, although he was fifteen years younger than her, she became his first wife and bore him six children.

The revelations to Muhammad ﷺ

By the time that he was 40 years old, Muhammad ﷺ spent much of his time praying and meditating in the desert. He was worried by the idolatrous behaviour of the people of Makkah, who worshipped 360 idols – of clay, wood and stone – which were kept in the **Ka'bah**, a shrine in the city. He was also disturbed by the gambling, drunkenness, violence and ill-treatment of the women and children in the city.

On 27 Ramadan 611 CE, Muhammad ﷺ was meditating in a cave near Hira when he had a vision of a superhuman being who ordered him to recite a text and called him 'the Messenger of God'. This text is now preserved as the 96th surah of the Qur'an. Muhammad ﷺ was convinced by his wife that the message had come from Allah. Further revelations followed and these now form the contents of the Qur'an.

When Muhammad ﷺ told others about his visions, the people of Makkah persecuted him and his growing band of followers. They all left Makkah to travel to Yathrib (now called **Madinah**) on a journey known to all Muslims as the **Hijrah** – 'emigration'. This journey was so important that Muslims date their calendar from this event.

The last years of Muhammad ﷺ

Muhammad ﷺ returned to Makkah with many followers and purged the Ka'bah of its idols. It became the centre of the worship of the one true God, Allah. His followers were told to always face towards this shrine when they were praying. This is still an important practice in Islam today. In each **mosque** there is a niche in the wall, the **mihrab**, which indicates the direction of Makkah and worshippers face it whenever they pray.

A number of battles were fought with the Makkans before the city was totally conquered. Muhammad ﷺ entered it with his followers to be proclaimed the Prophet of Allah. Ever since then, the city has been at the heart of Islam and every believer is expected to make a pilgrimage to the holy city once in their lifetime – called the Hajj. Muhammad ﷺ went on his last pilgrimage there in 632 CE and preached his last sermon there. As soon as he returned to Madinah, his health broke down and he died on 8 June 632 CE.

Muslims try to learn the Qur'an off by heart. If they do so, they are given the title of Hafiz.

The Qur'an

The **Qur'an**, the holy book for all Muslims, contains the revelations that Allah gave to Muhammad ﷺ. There are 114 **surahs** (divisions or chapters) and all of them, save one, begins with the words "In the name of Allah – All gracious, All merciful". In Arabic this is known as the **Bismillah** and is said by every Muslim before they do anything important. As the Qur'an is so highly revered, passages from it are learned by heart (Extract A) and used in prayers every day. Before reading, every Muslim must wash their hands thoroughly and, when it is not being used, the holy book is placed on a high shelf and covered with a cloth. Children are taught Arabic in their local religion school, called a **madraseh**, so that they can understand it when it is being read.

EXTRACT A

"*The best of you is he who has learnt the Qur'an and then taught it.*"

[The Prophet Muhammad ﷺ]

TO TALK ABOUT

Look at Extract A and try to work out why the Prophet Muhammad ﷺ linked together learning the Qur'an and teaching other people about it.

KEY WORDS

Allah – Bismillah – Hajj – Hijrah – Ka'bah – Khadijah – Madinah – Madraseh – Makkah – Mihrab – Mosque – Muhammad ﷺ – Prophet – Qur'an – Surah

Work

1. Describe the early life of the Prophet Muhammad ﷺ.
2. Describe how the people of Makkah treated the Prophet Muhammad ﷺ.
3. Write a paragraph about the Qur'an and explain how it is treated by Muslims.

A.16 Key Muslim beliefs (1)

KEY QUESTION What do Muslims believe about Allah?

Extract A from the Qur'an gives us a good summary of the most important Muslim beliefs. This topic, and Topic A.17, looks at the most important of these.

EXTRACT A
"*Believers, have faith in God and His apostle, in the Book He has revealed to His apostle, and in the Scriptures He formerly revealed. He that denies God, His angels, His Scriptures, His apostles, and the Last Day has gone far astray.*"

[Surah 4.136]

The 99 names of Allah

Islam provides worshippers with 99 of 'the most gracious' names of God. Male Muslims recite all of these names by running their fingers through 33 beads on their rosary three times. These beads, the **misbeha**, allow worshippers to choose a name for Allah which is most in keeping with the prayer they are saying. Reciting the 99 names in this way is an important devotional exercise since it makes the worshipper constantly aware of Allah's greatness.

EXTRACT B
"*He is God, besides whom there is no other deity. He knows the unknown and the manifest. He is the Compassionate, the Merciful. He is God, besides whom there is no other deity. He is the sovereign Lord, the Holy One, the Giver of Peace, the Keeper of Faith; the Guardian, the Mighty One, the All-powerful, the Most High! Exalted be God… His are the most gracious names…*"

[Surah 59.22–24]

Muslims believe that Allah is:

- one. This is the most important Muslim belief – it is called the **Tawhid**. God is One and there is no other god besides Him.
- supreme, eternal and omnipotent (all-powerful).
- all-seeing and present everywhere.
- the sole Creator and sustainer of the universe.
- the controller of the life and death of all His creatures.
- the provider of all good things for human beings to enjoy.
- all-knowing (omniscient).
- far beyond the reach of human understanding.

KEY WORDS

Allah – Holy Spirit – Jesus – Misbeha – Mosque – Muhammad – Qur'an – Shirk – Tawhid – Trinity – Virgin Mary

Shirk

The one unforgivable sin in Islam is that of 'association' – to deny God's sovereignty by associating Him with something or someone else. Muslims believe that Christians commit **shirk** when they worship Jesus, the Holy Spirit or the **Virgin Mary**. The Christian belief in the Trinity is blasphemous because it 'associates' other beings with God. All images, statues and pictures are strictly forbidden in a mosque for the same reason.

The Day of Judgement

The Day of Judgement on which all men and women will be called to account by Allah is a central theme in the Qur'an. On this day, all graves will be opened, the dead will return to life and all people will be sentenced by Allah according to how they have lived. Allah will hand them a book – if it is placed in their right hand they will pass into heaven and if it is placed in their left hand they will pass directly into hell.

Those who have lived charitable and faithful lives, together with those who have either fought or been persecuted for God's sake will enter heaven – with its beautiful gardens, flowing rivers, lovely serving maidens, heavenly food and reclining couches. The greatest joy for those in heaven will be to enjoy the eternal presence of Allah. For those in hell, however, their punishment will be eternal and never ending. The wicked will suffer fire and torment forever.

Muslim men use these beads, the misbeha, to help them remember the 99 names given to Allah in the Qur'an.

TO TALK ABOUT

Do you find it surprising that heaven and hell are spoken of in such graphic terms in the Qur'an? Do you believe in heaven and hell and, if so, how do you picture them?

Work

1. Write a list of the different beliefs that Muslims hold about Allah using Extract B to help you.
2. Explain what is meant by the word 'shirk'.
3. What do Muslims believe will happen on the Day of Judgement?

A.17 Key Muslim beliefs (2)

KEY QUESTION What are the Five Pillars of Islam?

The **Five Pillars** of Islam are the basic religious duties and responsibilities that each Muslim believer has. Taken together, the Five Pillars provide each believer with the basic framework for his or her life.

Pillar one – The confession of faith (the Shahadah)

The first pillar of Islam is known as the **Shahadah**. This simply says: "There is no god except God. Muhammad is the Messenger of God." Making this confession freely and with conviction officially makes a person a Muslim. The confession refers to the two basic teachings of Islam:

1. The Tawhid – the Oneness of Allah.
2. The uniqueness of Muhammad as the Prophet of Allah. This belief is known as the **Rusulullah**.

Pillar two – Prayer (Salah)

All Muslims, men and women, are required to pray five times each day: in the early morning; noon; mid afternoon; sunset; and at evening. Muslim prayer requires the ritual washing of the hands and face (called **wudu**), prostration in the direction of Makkah and other ritual movements. Usually the prayers are performed on a rug specially designed for the purpose.

On Fridays, public prayers are usually carried out in the mosque, although public prayers may be performed in the open air. Friday prayers are directed by an **imam**, a leader who has been set aside and trained for this purpose. The imam also delivers a sermon at this service.

Pillar three – Alms giving (Zakah)

Giving alms (gifts) helps to look after the economic welfare of the whole Muslim community. It requires that Muslims give 2.5% of the value of their possessions to the welfare of other Muslims. Poor people are exempt from this and receive help instead. This money can also be spent on public institutions such as schools and hospitals. Muslims consider that such wealth-sharing is part of worship, since it is sharing something that God has given in the first place with others who are less fortunate.

KEY WORDS

Allah – Five Pillars – Hajj – Imam – Ka'bah – Makkah – Mosque – Muhammad – Prophet – Ramadan – Rusulullah – Sawm – Shahadah – Tawhid – Ummah – Wudu – Zakah

Pillar four – Fasting (Sawm)

Muslims are expected to fast during the month of **Ramadan**, the ninth month of the Muslim year. Each day throughout that month, from dawn until sunset, Muslims avoid eating, drinking, smoking and sex. Some, however, are exempt from this requirement – the sick, the young, the elderly, those who are making difficult journeys and women who are breast-feeding. Muslims use a lunar calendar and so Ramadan moves through the different seasons over time. When it occurs during the very hot weather it presents a big challenge to a Muslim's commitment.

Prayer is one of the most important obligations placed on every Muslim man. Women also pray but their obligations to their family are more important.

Fasting has two spiritual benefits:

1. It gives wealthy Muslims an insight into the lives of those who are less fortunate.
2. It nurtures an awareness of mortality and focuses a person's attention on moral and spiritual, rather than material, values.

Pillar five – Pilgrimage to Makkah (the Hajj)

Once in their lifetime, if they can afford it and are physically fit, all Muslims make a journey to the city of Makkah. This journey, the **Hajj**, has great spiritual significance for Allah forgives the sins of those who undertake the journey with reverence. Any pilgrim who dies while making the pilgrimage is a martyr (a witness to the faith) and enters Paradise immediately.

The pilgrimage brings together pilgrims from all over the world to celebrate their common religion, regardless of their material differences. Male pilgrims wear plain white clothing and this shows their basic equality and their ritual purity. Female pilgrims wear simple, colourful clothing that reflects their own homeland. Brought together, the pilgrims enjoy experiencing the fellowship of the worldwide Muslim community – called the **Ummah**. The pilgrimage takes place in a specified month of the year and lasts just 15 days. It involves several ritual acts including walking around the Ka'bah seven times, as well as visits to other important sites in Islam.

Work

1. What is the Shahadah?
2. Describe and explain the importance of the following:
    a) Salah.   b) Sawm.   c) Zakah.
3. Use the Internet to find out some information about the Hajj. Draw up your own description of the pilgrimage to Makkah and find some comments from Muslims who have undertaken the journey.

A.18 THE ORIGINS OF JUDAISM

KEY QUESTION How did the religion of Judaism begin and grow?

Judaism, nearly 4,000 years old, is one of the oldest world religions. Its origins can be traced back to a group of people called the Israelites, who lived a nomadic life in a region now known as the Middle East.

The origins of Judaism

Although the people around him believed in many gods, Abraham came to believe in just one God. He felt sure that this God was calling him to leave his home in Haran, in modern Iraq, with his family to become the father of a great nation elsewhere – in the land of Canaan. Abraham was the first Jew. God made a promise to Abraham: "I will make you a great nation and I will bless you" (Genesis 12.2). This promise is known as the **covenant** and is the foundation of all Jewish faith in God. Abraham, together with his son, Isaac, and grandson, Jacob, are known as the patriarchs, or fathers, of Judaism.

Jacob's 12 sons became the leaders of the 12 tribes of **Israel**. Their story is told in the Jewish scriptures, the **Torah**. Jacob's favourite son, Joseph, was sold by his jealous brothers to some merchants and he ended up in Egypt – where he was sold as a slave. He rose to become an important official. A famine in Canaan led Jacob and his family to seek food in Egypt, where they became slaves. The Israelites remained slaves in Egypt for over 400 years.

To the Promised Land – and beyond

Nearly 300 years after the death of Joseph, God chose **Moses** to lead the Israelites out of Egypt, a journey known as the **Exodus**, and into the Promised Land of Canaan. On this journey, which lasted 40 years, the Israelites were given a set of laws which included the **Ten Commandments** (see Extract A). The Jewish scriptures described Canaan as a 'land flowing with milk and honey' and it was later renamed Israel.

> **EXTRACT A**
> "I am the Lord your God, who brought you out of the land of Egypt, out of the land of slavery. You shall have no other gods before me."
> [Exodus 20.2–3]

Later, the people asked God for a king. First Saul and then their much-loved monarch, **David**, were crowned. David's son, Solomon, built the most glorious temple in **Jerusalem** and the Jews tried to live their lives by the teaching of the Torah. They had their own kings, priests and prophets. God promised them peace and prosperity as long as they kept all of His laws and showed justice and mercy to all the inhabitants of Israel. Time and time again, however, they failed to live up to God's standards. The prophets criticised both kings and priests when they oppressed the poor and made bad laws.

Israel was now divided into two kingdoms – Israel and Judah. Israel fell in 721 BCE and Judah in 586 BCE. Many of the people living there were taken into exile after the temple was destroyed in Jerusalem in 586 BCE, but Israel was never to enjoy independence for long again. In 63 BCE it was invaded by the Romans and Jews were scattered throughout the world.

Each scroll of the Torah is copied out by a trained scribe by hand. If there is a single mistake, the scroll is destroyed and the work begins again.

The Jewish scriptures

The Jewish Bible consists of three groups of writing:

1. **The Torah.** The Torah, also known as the Five Books of Moses, is the most important of the holy books to Jews. Jews believe that the words of the Torah are the words of God revealed to Moses on Mount Sinai more than 3,000 years ago. As well as the early history of the Jewish religion, it gives instructions on every aspect of Jewish life. Religious Jews today show their commitment by still obeying these laws.
2. **The Prophets** (Nevi'im). These books continue the story of the Jews from the death of Moses. Included in this section are the books of Joshua, Judges, Samuel, Kings, Isaiah, Jeremiah and Ezekiel, as well as 12 shorter books.
3. **The Writings** (Ketuvim). Some of these books continue the history of the Jewish people – Esther, Daniel, Ezra and Nehemiah. The book of Psalms, with 150 songs used in temple worship, and the book of Proverbs, with its many witty sayings and pieces of advice are also included.

Key Words

Abraham – Covenant – David – Exodus – Israel – Jerusalem – Moses – Prophet – Ten Commandments – Torah – Writings

Exam tips

The holy books of the different religions are very important. Try to learn some extracts from them so that you can use them in your exam answers.

Work

1. a) Who is known as the 'father' of the Jewish people?
   b) Why do you think he is given this title?
2. How did the descendants of Abraham end up as slaves?
3. What is the Exodus and what happened on this journey?
4. What are the:
   a) Torah?   b) Prophets?   c) Writings?

A.19 Key Jewish Beliefs (1)

KEY QUESTION What do Jews believe about God?

Jews believe that they have a special relationship with God, based on the covenant that He made with Abraham in the Torah. This belief is at the heart of their religious faith.

◀ To show their respect for God, Jews cover their eyes when they reach the divine name as they recite the Shema.

The Shema

> **EXTRACT A**
> "Hear, O Israel! The Lord is our God, the Lord alone. You shall love the Lord your God with all your heart, and with all your soul and with all your might. Take to heart these instructions with which I charge you this day…"
>
> [Deuteronomy 6.4–5]

Extract A contains the opening words of the **Shema** ('Hear'). The full Shema is the most important Jewish prayer, as well as being a basic statement of Jewish belief. To underline its importance, Jews recite it every morning when they rise and in the evening before going to bed. It begins with the most important Jewish belief – that there is only one God. Abraham believed in one God who controlled everything and he passed this belief down to the Jewish people.

God is the creator and sustainer

The Jewish scriptures open with the words: "In the beginning, God created the heaven and the earth" (Genesis 1.1). The Jewish faith teaches that the universe did not create itself nor has it always existed. It is not the result of chance or an accidental collision of atoms. It was created by God since He is the source of all life. God created everything 'out of nothing' and He continues to pour His creative energies into the universe today. The universe is always changing – and that is the work of God.

Key Words

Abraham – Covenant – Messiah – Shema – Torah

To Talk About

Do you think there is a tension between the idea of God forgiving the failings of His people and God judging them?

God is omnipotent, omniscient and omnipresent

Jews believe that God is:

- **omnipotent (all-powerful)**. Although God is all-powerful, He holds back on that power so that people can freely choose whether to do right or wrong. An ancient Jewish saying says: "Wherever you find God's greatness, there you will find His humility." God does, however, use His power to help the Jewish people and there are many divine miracles recorded in the Jewish scriptures.
- **omniscient (all-knowing)**. God knows everything – what He has created and what He intends to create, the beginning and the end of history.
- **omnipresent (found everywhere)**. Jews strongly believe that the whole universe is filled with the presence of God.

God is the law-giver and judge

The Jewish scriptures stress the importance of the laws, the Torah, that God gave to the Jews. Jews believe that this was the greatest of all God's gifts to them. These laws made it clear that God expected a very high standard of moral and religious behaviour from the Jews. This is why God is portrayed as the righteous judge who will judge His people for their actions (Extract B).

This is part of the covenant agreement. If the Jews remain faithful to the demands of God's laws, then they can expect to enjoy His blessing. If they break that agreement, then they will be punished by God, the judge. After God's punishment, however, comes forgiveness.

The Jews were also encouraged to look beyond the present to the future. They expected God to send a promised **Messiah** or redeemer who would set up God's kingdom on earth. On that day God would begin to rule over the whole earth with fairness: "…He comes to judge the earth. He will rule the world justly and its people in faithfulness" (Psalm 96.13).

> **EXTRACT B**
> "Let the assembly of peoples gather about You, with You enthroned above, on high. The Lord judges the peoples; vindicate me, O Lord, for the righteousness and blamelessness that are mine."
> [Psalm 7.7–8, 11]

Work

1. What is the Shema and why is it important to every Jew?
2. What do we mean by describing God as:
   a) omnipotent?   b) omniscient?   c) omnipresent?
3. Describe why God is described in the Jewish scriptures as being the judge and the redeemer.

A.20 Key Jewish beliefs (2)

KEY QUESTION What are two important Jewish festivals and religious practices?

Here we are going to look at two Jewish festivals – Rosh Hashanah and Yom Kippur – and two religious practices which have a considerable effect on Jewish everyday life – Shabbat and Kashrut.

Rosh Hashanah and Yom Kippur

Rosh Hashanah (the Jewish New Year) and Yom Kippur (the Day of Atonement) are two Jewish festivals separated by just 10 days. On Rosh Hashanah, Jews believe that God judges His people for their actions over the past year and decides their future for the coming year. This is the day when God 'writes down' His final decision. This is why the prayers of Rosh Hashanah are addressed to God as a king sitting in judgement over the world. In the morning service, the **shofar**, a ram's horn, is sounded 100 times with three different notes being used to represent different kinds of crying to show the yearning of the people to be reunited with God.

> **EXTRACT A**
> "*Seek the Lord while He may be found.*" (Isaiah 5.6.) This refers to the ten days between Rosh Hashanah and Yom Kippur when God is closest to those who sincerely want to return to Him."
>
> [The Talmud]

Yom Kippur, the most solemn day in the Jewish year (Extract A), is the day when God closes the book and 'seals' His final decision about the fate of every Jew. On this day, Jews fast for 25 hours, during which they spend most of their time in the **synagogue** trying to make up (to atone) for their sins. People who know that they have committed a particular sin must make a special confession of it to the person most affected. At nightfall, a single blast on the shofar tells everyone that the fast has been completed and they can all return home.

Shabbat

Shabbat (the Sabbath Day) is the weekly day of rest for all Jews, beginning at sunset on the Friday evening and lasting until the stars appear on Saturday night. It is a holy day on which all work ceases so that each Jew is free to devote themselves to prayer and the study of the Torah. By resting on the Shabbat, Jews are showing that they believe God created the world and that after all His work He stopped to show that He would not create anything new (Genesis 2.1–3). The work of creation was completed. When they rest on Shabbat, Jews are following God's example.

Men begin Shabbat in the synagogue, where they greet the day as a bride coming to greet her husband. In the home, the mother, and her daughters, have prepared the table for a meal at which special foods are eaten.

Although many of the most important activities associated with Shabbat and the different Jewish festivals take place in the home, some time is almost always spent in the synagogue.

On the following morning everyone goes to the synagogue for a special service during which the Torah scroll is removed from the **Ark** and paraded around the synagogue. The day ends with the **Havdalah** ceremony during which four blessings are said and the separation of the holy day, the Shabbat, from the rest of the week is completed.

Kashrut

Kashrut is the name given to the Jewish dietary laws. It means the food that is 'fit' or 'correct' for Jews to eat. The laws cover both the foods that may and may not be eaten and also how those foods are to be prepared. The food which falls within the laws of kashrut are classified as **kosher** (fit or clean), while those that fall outside the laws are **treyfah** (unclean). Jews are allowed to eat:

- any animal that chews the cud and has divided hoofs – ruling out pigs and rabbits.
- any fish that has fins and scales.
- many birds such as duck, chicken and turkey, but not birds of prey.
- insects that hop.

Meat and milk dishes cannot be cooked together, nor can the same utensil be used to prepared meat and milk dishes. Most importantly, all blood must be drained out of an animal before it is eaten. Orthodox Jews try to run a kosher house, although Reform Jews sit easy on some of the rules.

Key Words

Ark – Havdalah – Kashrut – Kosher – Rosh Hashanah – Shabbat – Shofar – Synagogue – Torah – Treyfah – Yom Kippur

To Talk About

It seems likely that the kosher rules were first introduced for health reasons – reasons that do not apply in the modern age. Why do you think many Jews keep these dietary laws if they have lost their original purpose?

Work

1. Why are Rosh Hashanah and Yom Kippur the most solemn days in the Jewish year and how are they celebrated?
2. What do Jews remember on Shabbat and how do they celebrate the day?
3. What are the Kashrut rules?

A.21 THE ORIGINS OF SIKHISM

KEY QUESTION Who were the Ten Gurus and what part did they play in the origins of Sikhism?

Sikhism, the most recent of the major world religions, began in the 15th century in the Punjab, an area in northern India and Pakistan, and is based on the teachings of the **Ten Gurus**. The most important of the Gurus was the founder of Sikhism, **Guru Nanak**. In Eastern religions, a guru is a spiritual teacher while a Sikh is a learner or disciple – one who learns by following the teachings of a guru.

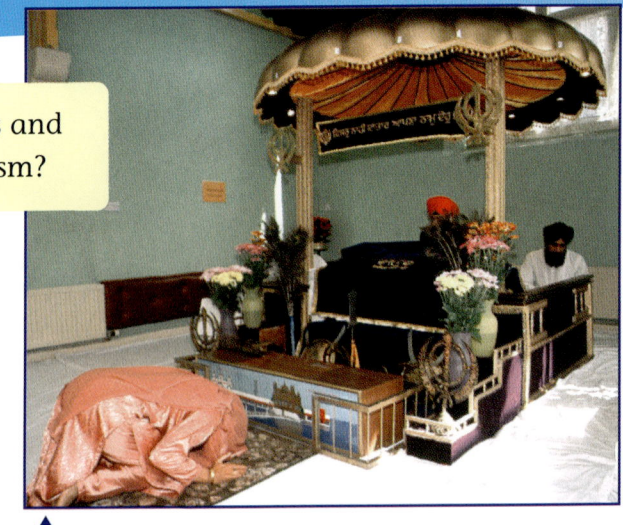

▲ Sikhs have come together to meet with each other in a gurdwara since the earliest days of their religion.

Guru Nanak

Guru Nanak (1469–1539) was born in a small village near Lahore, in present-day Pakistan. His family was Hindu and quite poor. He married in his teens and had two sons. At an early age he became very dissatisfied with Hinduism and sought help from a variety of holy men, both Hindu and Muslim. He strongly believed in the oneness of God and the need to move closer to God. Each morning he rose before dawn, bathed in the river, meditated and led others in singing praises to God. One day he had a revelation in which he was taken up into the court of God, who gave him a cup of nectar and told him to drink it. He was then sent back to earth to tell others about God.

Back on earth, Guru Nanak made several long preaching journeys over the next 20 years. He then set up a new township (Kartarpur) and formed the first Sikh community. He erected a special building, a **gurdwara**, and started to receive followers. About 20 years later, in 1539, he died.

Guru Angad and Guru Amar Das

Guru Angad (1504–1552) collected all the hymns of Guru Nanak and added some of his own. He developed Gurmukhi – the script in which the Sikh scriptures were finally written – by combining two older languages. To teach this new language to children, Guru Angad opened a school. Guru Amar Das (1479–1574) discovered that, when people visited Guru Nanak, they always sat down and ate together. This was an important way of teaching the basic lesson that all people were equal. To reinforce this, Guru Amar Das opened the first langar, or open kitchen, so that everyone who visited the Guru could sit down and eat first. The open kitchen is now a feature of every gurdwara.

Guru Ram Das and Guru Arjan

Guru Ram Das (1534–1581) founded the holy city of **Amritsar** in 1577 on land given by a Muslim emperor. He composed wedding hymns so that Sikhs no longer had to use the Hindu scriptures and priests when they married. Guru Arjan (1563–1606) gathered together the hymns written by the earlier Sikh Gurus, added some of his own, and published them as the **Adi Granth** ('First Book'). He became the first Sikh martyr.

The first and last of the Sikh Gurus – Nanak and Gobind Singh – still have a great influence on the faith today.

Guru Har Gobind; Guru Har Rai; Guru Har Krishan

Guru Har Gobind (1595–1644) taught Sikhs that they must be prepared to fight for their faith but he also cared greatly for their spiritual lives. He carried two swords – one to symbolise defending the faith and the other as a reminder of the spiritual struggle that everyone must fight. Guru Har Rai (1630–1661) encouraged the giving of free medicines and care to the sick. Guru Har Krishan (1656–1664) was only five when he became a guru and he died three years later from smallpox.

Guru Tegh Bahadur and Guru Gobind Singh

Guru Tegh Bahadur (1621–1675) died for his faith in preference to becoming a Muslim. **Guru Gobind Singh** (1666–1708) built the Sikh faith into a fighting force that could defend itself. He formed the Khalsa, the Sikh brotherhood, and you will find out more about this in Topic A.23. Guru Gobind Singh told his followers that he was to be the last of the human Gurus and said that the **Guru Granth Sahib**, the Sikh scriptures, would be the 'living guru' for the people in future. We will look at the central place given to the holy book in the life and worship of the Sikh community in Topic A.22.

Key Words

Adi Granth – Amritsar – Gurdwara – Guru – Guru Gobind Singh – Guru Granth Sahib – Guru Nanak – Khalsa – Langar – Ten Gurus

Exam tips

You should know some pieces of information about the most important Sikh Gurus – especially Guru Nanak, Guru Har Gobind and Guru Gobind Singh.

Work

1. Describe the life of Guru Nanak and the contribution that he made to the Sikh religion.
2. Write down *three* pieces of information about each of these Gurus:
    a) Guru Angad.   b) Guru Ram Das.   c) Guru Har Gobind.
3. Why was the death of Guru Gobind Singh particularly important?

A.22 THE GURU GRANTH SAHIB

KEY QUESTION What part does the Guru Granth Sahib play in Sikhism?

The death of Guru Gobind Singh in 1708 brought to an end the line of human Gurus who taught and led the Sikh community. Instead, from now on, all Sikhs were to be guided by the words of the Gurus which were recorded in the Guru Granth Sahib. The original name for this book, the Adi Granth ('that which is first and original'), indicates clearly its supreme importance for all Sikhs.

The importance of the Guru Granth Sahib

The original version of the holy book is an anthology which was compiled by the 5th Guru, Guru Arjan and placed in the **Harimandir**, the **Golden Temple** at Amritsar, in 1604. It was the last Guru, Gobind Singh, who later enthroned the book as the final Guru. The Guru Granth Sahib is a very large collection (1,430 pages) of poems, or hymns, which are placed in the 31 divisions, or melodies, in which they are intended to be sung. Each division begins with the **Mool Mantra** (Extract A), which is sung at morning and evening prayers in the gurdwara.

> **EXTRACT A**
> "There is one God, Eternal truth is his/her name, Creator of all things, Without fear, Without Emnity, Timeless, Immortal, Never incarnated, Beyond the cycle of birth and death, Self-created, Self-existent, Known by the grace of the Gurus."
> [The Mool Mantra]

The vast majority of the hymns were written by the different Gurus. The major contributor was Guru Arjan (2,218 hymns), followed by Guru Nanak (974 hymns) and Guru Amar Das (907 hymns). The holy book also contains hymns written by 36 other holy men from other parts of India and different religions. One Muslim, the poet Kabir, contributed 541 hymns. When Sikhs bow in front of the Guru Granth Sahib, therefore, they are recognising the wisdom that has been passed down by God through the followers of other religions as well as their own.

The teachings of the Guru Granth Sahib

The key to the Guru Granth Sahib, and all Sikh teaching, is the **Japji**. Found in the first section of the Guru Granth Sahib, this poem was written by Guru Nanak towards the end of his life. It is the only hymn in the Guru Granth Sahib which is recited and not sung. You can find a short extract in Extract B.

> **KEY WORDS**
> Adi Granth – Amritsar – Golden Temple – Granthi – Gurdwara – Guru Gobind Singh – Guru Granth Sahib – Guru Nanak – Harimandir – Japji – Karma – Mool Mantra – Nam – Ten Gurus – Waheguru

A building cannot be a gurdwara until a copy of the Guru Granth Sahib has been installed. It is the job of the **granthi** to make sure that it is treated with the proper respect.

There is a strong Sikh tradition that the teaching of one Guru reflected that of all the others – their forms changed but their 'lights' merged and the Guru's spirit remained the same through all of the authors. The same spirit inhabits the whole of the Guru Granth Sahib. This gives the holy book a unity that can be seen throughout all its teachings:

- There is only one God who is the Truth – the name of this God is **Nam**.
- There is a cycle of rebirth through which all souls pass, with the form that the next rebirth takes being determined by karma.
- Salvation can only be reached after a person meditates on God, repeats the divine name and then serves other people. God helps people to do this by providing them with the teachings of the Ten Gurus and the Guru Granth Sahib. Most people meditate on God's name by saying the Mool Mantra and repeating **Waheguru** (Wonderful Lord) over and over again.
- All people, male and female, are equal in the sight of God. Each person must work honestly, worship regularly in the gurdwara and give a tithe (a tenth of their income) to aid the poor.
- God does not recognise any differences between the different religions. When Guru Nanak returned from his vision of God in heaven he brought the message back with him that all religions are equal.

EXTRACT B

"*So pure is God's name, whoever obeys God knows the pleasure of it in his own heart. When the hands and the feet are covered with dirt, you remove it by washing with water. When the clothes are dirty, you clean them by washing with soap. So when the mind is defiled by sin, it is cleansed by the love of God's name.*"

[The Japji]

TO TALK ABOUT

The Sikh holy book has been called the 'final and immortal Guru'. What do think this phrase is telling us?

Work

1. What was the original name of the Guru Granth Sahib and what does its name tell us about the book?
2. Write a paragraph about the contents of the Guru Granth Sahib.
3. What are *four* of the teachings found in the Guru Granth Sahib?

A.23 Key Sikh beliefs

KEY QUESTION What is the Khalsa and what are the Five Ks?

Two key elements in Sikhism are the brotherhood founded by Guru Gobind Singh in 1699, the **Khalsa**, and the symbols which the members of the Khalsa wear – the **Five Ks**.

The Khalsa

A key event in the history of Sikhism took place at Baisakhi in 1699. Guru Gobind Singh asked for volunteers from the Sikh community who were prepared to die for their faith. Five men came forward and went into the Guru's tent one at a time. Each time, Guru Gobind Singh emerged with a blood-stained sword before bringing out all five men alive. He explained that these men had been willing to give up their lives for their faith, as all Sikhs should. They became the first members of the Khalsa, a community of men and women that unites Sikhs all over the world. Not all Sikhs belong to the Khalsa as it is a sign of real commitment to the faith.

The kirpan symbolises the spiritual warfare in which every member of the Khalsa is engaged.

Ever since 1699, the ceremony of initiation into the Khalsa has been performed by five men to represent the first members. Each initiate must be at least 14 years old and must possess the Five Ks (see below). The Adi Granth is opened and one of the five men explains the basic principles of the Khalsa. The initiates are asked if they accept them before being served with nectar made from water and sugar, which has been mixed in an iron kettle and stirred with a two-edged sword. The Mool Mantra is then recited. The four prohibitions that each member of the Khalsa is expected to observe are then read out:

1. Do not trim, cut or shave your hair.
2. Do not eat **halal** meat – meat that has been slaughtered according to Muslim or other religious regulations.
3. Do not engage in extramarital sexual relationships.
4. Do not smoke tobacco or drink any intoxicants.

The ideals of the Khalsa are very precious to its members. This is why the whole ceremony is held in front of an open copy of the Guru Granth Sahib.

The Five Ks

When Guru Gobind Singh started the Khalsa, he gave five symbols to the first people initiated into the brotherhood. At the time they had practical uses but now they are purely symbolic:

1. **The kesh (uncut hair).** This distinguishes Sikhs from all other groups in northern India. The kesh is a sign of their commitment to God. The hair is bunched up, fixed with a comb (kangha) and then bound up within a turban. Each Sikh is responsible for keeping his or her own hair clean.
2. **The kirpan (sword).** This can be up to three feet in length or much shorter. It expresses the power and the freedom to be found in Sikhism. Obviously, it did have practical value at some time but now it symbolises the spiritual warfare in which all members of the Khalsa are engaged. Sikhs in Britain are allowed to carry a kirpan because it is not considered to be an offensive weapon.
3. **The kangha (comb).** This should be used twice a day. Sikhs place a very high degree of importance on personal hygiene and their hair must be washed at least once every four days. If the long hair symbolises the spirituality which is at the heart of Sikhism, then the comb is a symbol of the discipline which is needed to keep that spirituality under control.
4. **The kara (steel bracelet).** A steel bangle that is worn on the right wrist. The circle itself is an important Sikh symbol and it forms part of the design on a Sikh flag. The bracelet is a constant reminder to the wearer that God is eternal and one; that the unity between God and a believer is never ending and so is the unity that binds one Sikh to another.
5. **The kachs (shorts).** Hindu holy men wore long cloaks and these were clearly impractical for fighting. By wearing shorts, a Sikh shows that he is always ready to take up arms to defend his religion. They symbolise discipline and readiness, while their modesty indicates sexual discipline.

TO TALK ABOUT

The Khalsa ceremony is often called 'baptism by the sword'. Can you think of any reason for this?

The circle of the bracelet, the kara, reminds members of the Khalsa of the infinity of God.

Key Words

Adi Granth – Five Ks – Guru Gobind Singh – Guru Granth Sahib – Halal – Kachs – Kesh – Khalsa – Kirpan – Mool Mantra

Work

1. How did Guru Gobind Singh set up the Khalsa?
2. Write down *five* things that happen in the Khalsa ceremony.
3. What are the Five Ks and what do they symbolise?

A.24 Sikh worship

KEY QUESTION What are the characteristics of Sikh congregational worship?

Guru Nanak encouraged his followers to reject many of the religious practices associated with Hinduism and Islam. He regarded what he called 'the external forms of religion' as useless. Instead, he encouraged people to focus on seeking God within themselves by meditating on God's name.

Services in the gurdwara provide an opportunity for people to meditate on the name of God.

Individual worship

Each day Sikhs rise early, take a bath and recite some verses from the Adi Granth, including the Japji. They end each day by reciting the words of two hymns – the Rahiras and the Sohila. The Sikh prayer, the **Ardas**, draws each day to a close. Most Sikh households have a selection of hymns normally recited during private worship (the **gutka**), wrapped in a cloth and kept in a safe place. Few families have their own copy of the Guru Granth Sahib as it would need to be kept in its own room at the top of the house.

The purposes of congregational worship

Congregational worship takes place in the gurdwara. A gurdwara can be any building with a copy of the Guru Granth Sahib properly installed. There is no fixed day for worship, although outside India it is usually held on a Sunday. Sikh worship has three main purposes:

1. To provide an opportunity for worshippers to read and meditate on the words of the Guru Granth Sahib. This is the only opportunity that most Sikhs have to study the holy book.
2. To bring Sikhs together into a community where they can join together in singing hymns of praise to God.
3. To show unity and equality, which are so highly prized in the Sikh community.

Worship in the gurdwara

Before visiting a gurdwara to worship, either in the morning or the evening, Sikhs always bathe. Before entering the building, worshippers touch the flagpole, touch the step and then, with the same hand, touch their forehead. This is in accordance with the words of the Guru Granth Sahib: "Wherever my Sat Guru goes and sits, that place is beautiful, O Lord King. The guru's disciples seek that place and take and apply its dust to their foreheads."

> The preparation and the eating of food give everyone the opportunity to serve other members of the Sikh community.

The service of worship lasts for several hours, during which people are free to come and go freely. They are expected, however, to be in the gurdwara as the service draws to a close. The service is mainly made up of the singing of **kirtan** (hymns), which is accompanied by musicians playing hand drums and a harmonium. During the service, there is time for meditation on God's name and saying the Mool Mantra.

An important moment in the service is reached when the Guru Granth Sahib is opened at random and a reading is given, starting at the top left-hand corner of the page. This reading is given the name of **Hukam** – the will of God. Each worshipper is seeking to know God's will through this random reading. The service closes with a final hukam to give the people a thought to take with them into the coming week. The service concludes with the recital of the Ardas prayer, read by the granthi (reader of the scripture) while the congregation stands silently with folded arms.

The service ends with the distribution of holy food (**karah parshad**) to the members of the congregation. This symbolises the Sikh belief in the equality of humankind.

The langar

Once the service has finished, everyone eats a communal meal in the **langar**. The food is strictly vegetarian and may be eaten standing or sitting – as long as everyone is doing the same. The food has been provided by members of the congregation and is cooked during the service by volunteers. It is traditionally eaten with the right hand only. The kitchen is free and everyone, Sikh and non-Sikh, is encouraged to share in it. The spiritual value of the meal is that it is a practical experience of sharing. Finally, the Guru Granth Sahib is carried out of the gurdwara above the heads of everyone present.

To Talk About

Why do you think that Sikhism, and other religions, continually suggest that physical cleanliness is necessary before spiritual cleansing?

Key Words

Adi Granth – Ardas – Granthi – Gurdwara – Guru Granth Sahib – Guru Nanak – Gutka – Hukam – Japji – Karah parshad – Kirtan – Langar – Mool Mantra

Work

1. How are Sikhs expected to worship God at home?
2. Why do few Sikhs have a copy of the Guru Granth Sahib in their own house?
3. What are the *three* purposes of Sikh worship?
4. What are the main characteristics of a service of worship in a Sikh gurdwara?
5. Define, in a sentence, the meaning of each of the following:
    a) Gurdwara.   b) Hukam.   c) Langar.

A.25 Christian decision-making

> **KEY QUESTION** What sources of help do Christians use when they have a moral decision to make?

We all use various sources of advice when we have important decisions to make. As young people we are likely to consult our parents, our teachers, our friends, our siblings (brothers and sisters) and possibly the magazines we read. When we are older, we are most likely to talk it over with our spouse and friends, consult any books that we trust or even look up information on the Internet. In addition, Christians might consult the following:

> Most Christians find guidance in making moral decisions from reading their Bible.

The Bible

The Bible does not provide a ready-made answer to all of the problems that confront Christians in the 21st century. All of its books were written, after all, about 2,000 years ago, at a time when problems such as abortion, euthanasia, drug-taking and damage to the environment did not exist. Christians, though, may find some direct help in the Bible on such issues as using money, sexual behaviour and other general aspects of behaviour. Most Christians would accept the teaching of Jesus to "Love your neighbour as yourself" as a principle to guide them through life.

Church traditions and teachings

Church traditions have built up over the centuries and they are much more important to some Christians than others. The Roman Catholic Church, for example, places a high degree of importance on tradition. It is a tradition of the Roman Catholic Church that the Apostle Peter was the first Bishop of Rome and **Pope**. This tradition means that the present Pope carries the same authority as the first holder of that office – and so speaks with God's authority on a whole variety of issues such as contraception, abortion and euthanasia. Christians from other churches, however, do not accept the authority of the Pope in the same way.

Churches and Christians do not always agree on the large moral issues. Some Christians will seek the advice of their minister or priest before they take an important decision. He or she will reflect on how their own church or denomination approaches the issue. Some churches, notably the Roman Catholic Church, see such moral issues as abortion and euthanasia in very 'black and white' terms. Others, such as the **Methodist Church** and the **Church of England**, are less clear cut.

Prayer

Prayer plays a larger role in the everyday lives of some Christians than others. Some Christians believe that 'prayer changes things' and that God has a plan for their life. If so, then prayer is the way to discover just what that plan is. Others believe, however, that prayer is a way of stilling their hearts so that they can hear 'the still, small voice of God'.

Reason

Human beings are thinking creatures and it is this, more than anything else, which makes them different from all other animals. Everyone should try to work out the consequences of taking a particular course of action and take them into account before making a decision. Very often this will make the right course to take clear. Christians are no exception to this rule.

Conscience

Most Christians believe that God's Holy Spirit speaks to them and guides them through their conscience. This gives them their sense of what is right and wrong.

The examples of others

Many people in recent years, such as Nelson Mandela and Desmond Tutu, have inspired Christians to oppose such attitudes as racism. Others find themselves inspired by characters in the Bible. For Christians, the supreme example must always be that of Jesus.

Work

1. How might a Christian find help from the Bible when trying to decide the right and wrong thing to do?
2. How might Church tradition help a Roman Catholic?
3. How might Christians find the examples of others helpful?

KEY WORDS

Abortion – Bible – Church of England – Holy Spirit – Jesus – Roman Catholic Church – Methodist Church – Peter – Pope

TO TALK ABOUT

Christians follow the Bible, church teachings, prayer, reason, their conscience and the examples of others in making moral decisions. Imagine that you are a Christian and place these different guides in what you would consider to be their order of importance. Explain your answer.

Christians understand prayer to be a means of communicating with God – and hearing God respond to them. This helps them in their decision-making.

A.26 Four kinds of love

KEY QUESTION What is Christian love?

We are going to look at four different kinds of love and three passages from the Bible, which can help us to understand just what that love is. Christians agree that love is at the heart of the message of their faith. It is the basis of the nature of God (God is love); the relationship between God and the universe; the relationship between God and the human race (see Extract A); the relationship between God and the Church; and the relationship between human beings. Christians believe that all human love reflects the love of God.

▲ Most people would think that this mother is showing the deepest love of which human beings are capable.

EXTRACT A
"*For God loved the world so much that he gave his only Son, so that everyone who believes in Him may not die but have eternal life.*"

[John 3.16]

The four kinds of love

In the New Testament there are four different kinds of love, each of which is indicated by a different Greek word:

1 **Agape**. This is Christian love and has little to do with the emotional feelings that we normally associate with love. This is a love which shows itself through caring and thoughtful actions. It reaches out to others in need – whether or not we will be loved in return. It shows a tolerance and respect for the feelings and needs of others. Two examples of this love in the New Testament are the story of the Good Samaritan (Luke 10.25–37) and the early Christians selling all their possessions to share the proceeds with the poor (Acts 2.43–47).

2 **Eros**. This is a very different kind of love to agape. It is sexual love and all the emotions that we link to it – passion, desire and lust. Paul discusses sex and marriage in 1 Corinthians 7 but this kind of love does not play an important part in the New Testament.

3 **Philia**. This is the kind of love that two friends have for each other. It is the feeling that Paul had for Timothy, whom he described as: "…my true son in the faith" (1 Timothy 1.2).

4 **Storge**. This is a love for things rather than people, a warm affection or deep liking. When the rich young ruler enquired about entering God's kingdom, he was told that his wealth stood in the way because he loved it so much (Luke 18.18–30).

Three passages from the New Testament

Mark 12.28–34
A teacher of the Law wondered which was the most important commandment of all – Jesus replied that it was to love God with all your heart, soul, mind and strength. He went on to the second greatest commandment – to love your neighbour as you love yourself. The teacher was greatly impressed by the answer of Jesus and agreed with him totally. Jesus had summed up the very essence of Christianity – nothing matters besides loving God, loving others and loving yourself without reservation.

1 Corinthians 13
Paul is describing the true qualities of Christian agape love here. He says that it is patient; kind; not jealous, conceited or proud; is not ill-mannered, selfish or irritable; does not keep a record of wrongs; is not happy with evil but is happy with the truth; does not give up; and its faith, hope and patience do not fail. Love is eternal. These words are often read at Christian wedding services.

Matthew 5.43–48
This is a love that breaks down barriers between enemies. It is the difference between the old way of doing things: "You have heard that it was said, 'Love your friends and hate your enemies'" (Matthew 5.43) and the new way, the way of Jesus: "…love your enemies and pray for those who persecute you, so that you may become the children of your Father in heaven." (Matthew 5.44.)

Even pagan non-believers in God are happy to love those who love them but Christian love is different – it loves those who are unloving in return.

Key Words

Bible – Church – Jesus – New Testament – Paul

Exam tips

When a reference is given to a passage in the Bible, it is very important to read it before you read the comments in the book about it.

Work

1. Explain the differences between agape, eros, philia and storge.
2. How did Jesus describe the *two* most important of God's commandments?
3. What are some of the qualities of love described by Paul?
4. What reasons did Jesus give for his followers loving their enemies?

A.27 Christian love and forgiveness

KEY QUESTION What can we learn from the New Testament about love and forgiveness?

Here we are going to look at three passages from the Gospels. The first, the story of the Good Samaritan, illustrates true Christian love in action. The second account, a woman caught in an act of adultery, shows that no one is beyond the reach of God's forgiveness. In the third story, the parable of the unforgiving servant, Jesus explains that those who want to be forgiven by God must be prepared to forgive others who have wronged them first.

The Good Samaritan (Luke 10.25–37)

A lawyer tried to trap Jesus into saying the wrong thing when he asked the question: "Teacher, what must I do to receive eternal life?" Jesus replied by asking the man what the Scriptures said and received the answer: "Love the Lord your God with all your heart, with all your soul, with all your strength, and with all your mind." Jesus commended the man for his answer and said that he had found the secret of eternal life. The lawyer, however, had not finished and wanted to know who his neighbour was. Jesus answered by telling his most well-known parable. The story makes three points:

1. The Jews and the Samaritans were sworn enemies and had been for centuries. The Good Samaritan was a very unlikely hero for a story told by a Jew.
2. Two people who would have been expected to have been the heroes of the story are said to have passed the injured man by on the other side of the road – a priest and a Levite.
3. Agape love, Christian love, demands that we help everyone in need – even those who are our traditional enemies. The person 'in need' is our true 'neighbour'.

The woman taken in adultery (John 8.1–11)

This was a very difficult situation for Jesus to face. The Jewish scriptures laid down the rule that adulterers should be stoned (Leviticus 20.10), although, as far as we know, this was rarely done. Clearly, Jesus could not deny the teaching of the Jewish scriptures as that would give his enemies very powerful ammunition to use against him. He bent down and began to write with his finger in the sand – we do not know why he did so or what he wrote. His answer, however, was much to the point – he invited anyone who was without sin themselves to throw the first stone. One by one the woman's accusers melted away. Jesus forgave the woman for her sin and told her to go on her way and to sin no more. Jesus was teaching her, and her accusers, that everyone is in need of God's mercy and forgiveness.

The Good Samaritan – a story told by Jesus to answer the question, 'Who is my neighbour?'

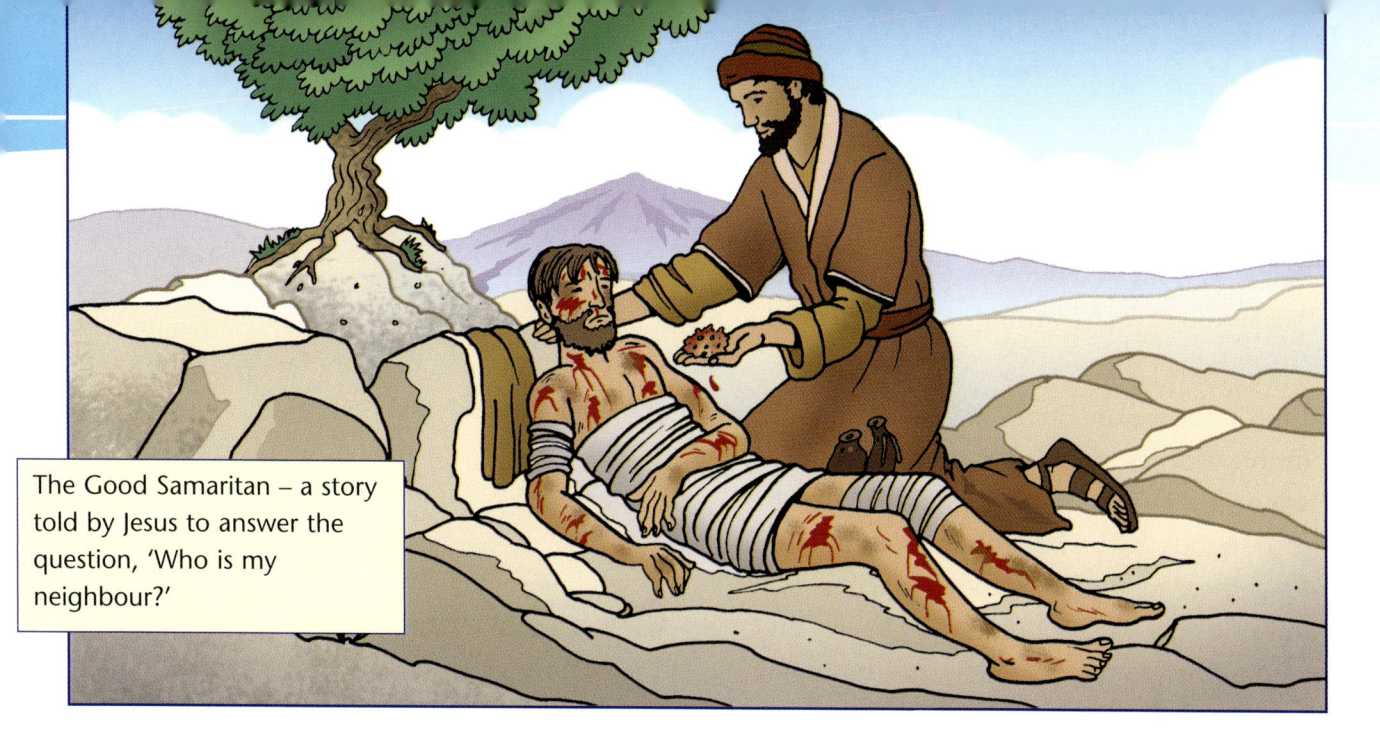

The unforgiving servant (Matthew 18.21–35)

This parable of Jesus is introduced to answer a question put to him by Peter, his most prominent disciple. Peter wondered how many times he should forgive a fellow disciple if he continued sinning against him. Peter thought he was being generous if he forgave the man seven times. Jesus told him that he should be prepared to forgive without limit. He then told him the story of the servant who was forgiven a huge debt by his master but who then refused to forgive a fellow servant a much smaller debt. For this, he was thrown into prison by his master and left there until he paid back the original debt in full.

The story was intended to teach two lessons:

1. God is the master in the parable. He is ready to forgive all those who are in debt to Him and to cancel their debt in full. There is no limit to God's forgiveness.
2. God's forgiveness depends on the forgiven person's willingness to forgive others and to cancel their debts. This shows God's readiness to forgive and also His justice. Unless His followers forgive one another, they will be held to account by God – and punished until their debts are paid in full.

Key Words

Gospel – Jesus – New Testament – Parable – Peter

To Talk About

What do you think Christians today might learn from the parable of the Good Samaritan?

Work

1. What question was Jesus asked to which he responded with the parable of the Good Samaritan?
2. Tell the story of the Good Samaritan and point out why the parable may have taken listeners by surprise.
3. How did Jesus make the accusers of the woman taken in adultery steal away in shame?
4. What can we learn from the story of the unforgiving servant about forgiveness?

A.28 Jesus and Forgiveness

KEY QUESTION What can we learn from Jesus about God's willingness to forgive our sins?

In this topic we are going to look at one further parable that Jesus told with forgiveness as its theme – that of the prodigal son. We are also going to look at the healing of the paralysed man, where healing and the forgiveness of the man's sins are closely linked. Finally, we are going to look at the death of Jesus and what Christians believe to be its significance.

▲ The Gospels tell us that the Roman soldiers made a crown of thorns for Jesus to mock his claim to be 'king of the Jews'.

The prodigal son (Luke 15.11–32)

Luke grouped together three parables of Jesus – the lost sheep, the lost coin and the lost son – with a common theme. Jesus explained to his listeners that he had come to rescue those who had lost their way in life. The parable of the lost son is the most important of the three parables and its three main characters are all symbolic:

1. The father who 'loses' his son but never gives up hope is a symbol for God the Father. The father watches out each day for the son's return and is overjoyed when he sees his son in the distance returning home. He gives him the best possible reception and asks no questions. He even throws a big welcome-home party! This is the welcome that God gives the sinner who has spent much time away from Him but returns home asking for forgiveness.
2. The prodigal, younger, son who returns home asking for forgiveness is the sinner who returns to God.
3. The older son who objects to the welcome that his younger brother is given symbolises the religious leaders who, Jesus insisted, prevented others from entering God's kingdom.

The paralysed man (Matthew 9.1–8)

Jesus was confronted by a paralysed man who was carried to him by some friends. Jesus was much impressed by the faith of the friends and he told the man that his sins had been forgiven. This was significant. In those days, most people believed that physical suffering and illness was the direct result of a person's sins – or those of the parents. The problem was that only God could forgive sins – and Jesus was plainly claiming to be God's Son here.

Jesus replied that he would prove his authority to forgive sins by healing the man. He told the man to pick up his bed and go home – and he did. We are not given any answer to the question of whether the man was paralysed because of his sins, but the incident does teach us that Jesus had the power to heal and that, as God, he also had the authority to forgive sins.

The death of Jesus (Luke 23.26–43)

After Pontius Pilate had passed the death sentence, Jesus was led away to be crucified. He was too weak to carry his own cross and so a bystander, Simon of Cyrene, was forced by the soldiers to step in. The group was followed by women onlookers who were weeping and wailing. Two other criminals were also led out at the same time to be crucified. On the cross, Jesus asked for God's forgiveness on those who were carrying out the crucifixion: "Forgive them, Father! They do not know what they are doing." One of the criminals executed with Jesus asked to be remembered when Jesus returned to set up his kingdom on earth: "Jesus said to him, 'I promise you that today you will be in Paradise with me.'"

Christians believe that Jesus voluntarily surrendered his own life so that the sins of the world could be forgiven. Jesus was sinless and so he could not be dying because he deserved the punishment. God could only forgive sins if a perfect sacrifice was made and Jesus, alone, could provide that. Christians believe that, in dying, Jesus made the forgiveness of the whole world possible.

Christians believe that the death of Jesus was the supreme example of God's love, making their own forgiveness by God possible.

Key Words
Gospel – Jesus – Parable

To Talk About
What do you think Christians today can learn about forgiveness from the parable of the prodigal son?

Work

1. What is the symbolic significance of the *three* characters in the story of the prodigal son?
2. Why did Jesus upset the religious leaders with his opening words to the paralysed man?
3. How did Jesus demonstrate his willingness to forgive others in the last few minutes of his life?
4. What do Christians believe to be the significance of the death of Jesus?

Exam questions

Question 1 – Buddhism
1. Describe a legend associated with the birth of the Buddha.
2. Describe what happened when Siddattha Gotama was enlightened.
3. Explain the importance of the Eightfold Path.
4. How do Buddhists show their devotion to the Buddha and his teachings?
5. "Buddhists do not believe in God so they do not worship as other religious believers do." Do you agree with this statement? Give reasons for your answer.

Question 2 – Christianity
1. Write down *four* things that we know about the life and work of Jesus.
2. What do Christians mean when they say that they believe in the Trinity?
3. What do the incidents of the rich young ruler and Zacchaeus say about eternal life?
4. Explain the link between the last meal that Jesus celebrated with his disciples and the service of Holy Communion.
5. "Christians agree about the meaning of Holy Communion." Do you agree with this statement? Give reasons for your answer.

Question 3 – Hinduism
1. Which *three* gods make up the Trimurti? Write *two* sentences about each of them.
2. Write *four* sentences about:
   a) shruti.
   b) smriti.
3. Write notes on *four* different Hindu gods.
4. What do Hindus mean by 'ahimsa'?
5. "The home and not the shrine in the vihara is the most important place for Hindu worship." Do you agree with this statement? Give reasons for your answer.

Question 4 – Islam
1. What does the word 'Islam' mean?
2. Write down *three* things that Muslims believe about God.
3. Write down *three* things that Muslims believe about life after death.
4. What are the Five Pillars of Islam?

Question 5 – Judaism
1. Who is known as the 'father of the Jewish people'?
2. What do Jews mean when they refer to the 'covenant'?
3. Write notes on the Jewish scriptures.
4. Describe *five* things that happen on Rosh Hashanah or Yom Kippur.
5. "Shabbat is a very important weekly Jewish festival." Do you agree with this statement? Give reasons for your answer.

Question 6 – Sikhism
1. What happened at Baisakhi in 1699?
2. Describe *four* teachings found in the Guru Granth Sahib.
3. Briefly describe the beginnings and the importance of the Khalsa.
4. Explain the importance of *three* of the Five Ks.
5. "Sikh congregational worship is more important than worship at home." Do you agree with this statement? Give reasons for your answer.

Question 7 – Christian ethics
1. Describe *two* kinds of love found in the New Testament.
2. Describe *three* sources of guidance and advice that Christians might use.
3. What can be learned about Christian love and forgiveness from:
   a) the parable of the Good Samaritan?
   b) the incident involving the woman taken in adultery?

Section B
Questions of Meaning

In this section you will find out about:

B.1 Believing in God or not

B.2 The argument for God's existence from design in the world

B.3 The argument for God's existence from religious experience

B.4 The teachings of Buddhism, Christianity and Hinduism about God

B.5 The teachings of Islam, Judaism and Sikhism about God

B.6 The problem of suffering and belief in God

B.7 Two important questions about suffering

B.8 The teachings of Buddhism, Christianity and Hinduism about suffering

B.9 The teachings of Islam, Judaism and Sikhism about suffering

B.10 Whether there is any reason to believe in a life after death

B.11 The teachings of Buddhism, Christianity and Hinduism about life after death

B.12 The teachings of Islam, Judaism and Sikhism about life after death

B.13 The link between believing in life after death and living today

B.1 THE EXISTENCE OF GOD

KEY QUESTION What is the cosmological proof for the existence of God?

It is not easy to prove that anything exists – least of all God! To satisfy themselves that there is a God, people draw on:

1. Their own personal experience – "I know that God exists because I have experienced Him myself."
2. The personal experiences of others – "I know that God exists because many other people believe that they have experienced Him and I believe them."
3. Common sense – "I have not experienced God but, if I believe, the chances are that He does exist."

The problem with approaches 1 and 2 is that we can never be sure that our own experience, or that of others, has been of God. We could all so easily be mistaken. The problem with approach 3 is that it may just be wishful thinking on our part.

People fall into three groups when deciding whether God exists or not:

1 The atheist

The **atheist** rejects any possibility that there is a God (Extract A). The scientist is able to answer all of our questions about the universe and life, or will soon be able to. There is no place for God in any scientific explanation.

2 The agnostic

The **agnostic** believes that there is no convincing argument that makes a belief of God necessary – or unnecessary. At the moment, the jury is out on this issue and the only sensible thing to do is to wait until the available evidence becomes clearer – one way or the other. This is unlikely to happen in one short lifetime.

3 The theist

Theists are people who are convinced that God does exist because they:

- believe that they have had a personal experience of God, or
- have come into contact with people who claim to have experienced God through joining a religious community – whether a church, synagogue, mosque, vihara or a gurdwara, or
- have decided that the 'ultimate questions' of life cannot possibly be answered without believing in God. Theists believe that everything has a purpose – God's purpose.

EXTRACT A

"*Fools say to themselves, 'There is no God.' They are all corrupt, and they have done terrible things; there is no one who does what is right.*"

[Psalm 14.1]

Many people find it necessary to offer up religious worship but those who do not believe in God find this very difficult to understand.

The Cosmological (First Cause) argument

This is one of the traditional 'proofs' for the existence of God. It uses the existence of the world (the cosmos) to prove that God must exist. This argument was first put forward by St Thomas Aquinas, a 13th century philosopher, who argued like this:

- Everything exists because someone or something has brought it into existence. Nothing can bring itself into existence. Everything has a cause.
- The universe exists.
- Something or someone must have brought the universe into existence.
- Only God, the First Cause or the Uncaused Cause, could have created the universe. God is the only exception to the rule that everything has a cause. God has always existed.

Many people are not convinced by this argument for two main reasons:

1. If God created the world, who created God? This is the obvious question and remains unanswered. It is not good enough to simply say that God is the only exception to the rule that everything must have a cause.
2. Just because everything else has a cause, this does not mean that the universe must have a cause. The universe could be eternal and at least one religion, Hinduism, teaches this.

TO TALK ABOUT

Would you describe yourself as being an atheist, an agnostic or a theist? Give some reasons for the point of view that you hold.

KEY WORDS

Agnostic – Atheist – Church – Gurdwara – Mosque – Synagogue – Theist – Vihara

Work

"There is no evidence for the existence of God." Do you agree with this statement? Give reasons for your answer, showing that you have considered more than one point of view.

B.2 The Argument from Design

KEY QUESTION What is the teleological proof for the existence of God?

> **EXTRACT A**
> "Ever since God created the world, His invisible qualities, both His eternal power and His divine nature, have been clearly seen; they are perceived in the things that God has made."
>
> [Romans 1.20]

Theists point to the order and design that they find in the natural world to prove that God must exist. This is called the Teleological argument, taken from the Greek word 'telos' meaning 'order'. It was an argument first suggested in the New Testament (see Extract A).

Paley's watch

The Teleological argument for God's existence was put forward in the 18th century by William Paley. He suggested that the evidence for design in the universe was one of the strongest reasons for believing in God. His argument fell into two parts:

1. Paley said that, if a man suddenly found a beautiful watch with its intricate balancing wheels and mechanism, what would he think? That it had come into existence by accident? No! That it had always existed? No! That it had been made by a skilled watchmaker? Yes! Only a watchmaker who understood all about watches could have made the watch.

2. The universe is a far more complicated piece of machinery than a watch. We can discover this by looking at the animals, birds and the infinite variety of human beings that are on earth. Something as intricate as the universe must have an eternal and infinite creator behind it – God. In the story of creation in the book of Genesis, God created the universe with a clear purpose in His mind – and it shows. Its clear purpose is to sustain all forms of life and everything in the universe is designed with that in mind.

The Anthropic Principle

In the 1930s, F. R. Tennant, a philosopher, took Paley's argument a step further. He argued that God had created the earth with everything in place so that the animal and human life could develop – by evolution. The balance of everything throughout the universe was such that life could begin and develop. A slight variation in any part of the equation, such as in the law of gravity, and life would have been impossible. This balance was clearly deliberate and shows a very clear sense of purpose.

Theists believe that the existence of different animals shows that there is evidence for design in the natural world.

Against design

It is a very beautiful and breathtaking world in which we live. Everything does seem to have been purposefully planned – until we look at life more closely:

- Science tells us that the world was the result of a cosmic Big Bang which took place about 15 million years ago. This was a random event and not a deliberate purposeful act by God.
- Evolution tells us that life is governed by the principle of natural selection – the fittest survive and the weakest die. Charles Darwin, who first explained evolution in the 19th century, described nature as being 'red in tooth and claw'. Those creatures which have not successfully adapted to the changing conditions of life have become extinct, as the dinosaurs so graphically illustrate. Similarly, many creatures in the modern world are now under threat because they are not well designed for their changing environment. Cruelty is as much a feature of life as beauty.
- If God created life with a clear purpose in mind, why allow pain, poverty, disease, typhoons, wars and a range of destructive natural events? It doesn't make any sense.
- The 'order' that appears in the universe could just as easily be the result of evolution and natural selection as that of a grand design.

Key Words

Theist – New Testament

Exam tips

Remember, it is important not to waffle in any of your exam answers. You can only be given marks for the facts that you give to the examiner and the use you make of them.

Work

1. What did William Paley say about:
    a) the watch?   b) the universe?
2. What is the Anthropic Principle and what does it add to William Paley's Teleological argument for God's existence?
3. List *four* objections that could be raised against the Teleological argument.

B.3 Experiencing God

KEY QUESTION Why do many people claim to have experienced God?

Religious people believe that God can reveal Himself to them, and others, in a variety of different ways. It might be through reading a holy book; through worshipping in a holy building; through having an overwhelming experience of nature's beauty; or simply through common, everyday experiences. By whatever means, many people believe that they have experienced God.

Experiencing God through conversion

The holy books are full of examples where someone has been moved to change the whole direction of their life through a sense that they have encountered God. Here are one or two examples:

- After meditating underneath the bodhi tree, and rejecting the temptations of Mara, Siddattha Gotama was enlightened.
- It was on the road to Damascus that Saul, a persecutor of the early Christians, heard a voice from heaven speaking to him. His story, told in the New Testament, describes how Saul became Paul – the early leader of the Christian Church and a tireless missionary.
- Hindu holy men (**sannyasin**) give up worldly pleasures and luxuries because they believe that they have experienced the reality of God.
- It was while he was meditating in the cave at Hira, that the angel Jibril revealed to Muhammad that he was to be the last, and greatest, of Allah's prophets.
- God revealed himself to Moses in a bush that was on fire but was not burned by the flames.
- Guru Nanak was taken to heaven to receive a revelation from God before he became the founder of Sikhism.

Great religious teachers, as well as millions of followers of the different religions, claim to have experienced God. These experiences changed the whole direction that their lives were taking. This is what the word 'conversion' means.

Experiencing God through a miracle

A 'miracle' is an event which cannot be explained rationally. There are some well-documented cases of miracles taking place, although few people would claim to have experienced one. Occasionally, you will hear of people being cured by a miracle and miracles of this nature are reported in all of the major religious traditions.

Religious believers make holy journeys (called 'pilgrimages') to holy places where they believe that miracles have occurred in the past. Over two million Catholic pilgrims each year, for example, travel to Lourdes, in south-west France, where, it is believed, the Virgin Mary appeared to a young peasant girl in the middle of the 19th century.

Experiencing God through prayer and worship

Many religious believers claim that they experience God through worship. Many Christians, especially those in Charismatic churches, believe that they are filled and led by the Holy Spirit in their worship and their daily lives. In Pentecostal churches some people 'speak in tongues' – an unknown language given to them by God particularly for intimate fellowship and prayer with him.

Other Christians find that their worship based on the sacraments provides them with symbols which make the worship of God meaningful.

Sometimes a mystical (spiritual) experience is part of prayer. Some people, for example, use 'imaging' when they pray. They take an image from the Gospels, such as Jesus teaching the crowds or feeding the 5,000, to help them to enter into the experience for themselves.

This Hindu holy man, a sannyasin, has devoted his life to seeking closer contact with God in the hope that he can escape from the cycle of birth, death and rebirth.

Key Words

Allah – Gospel – Guru Nanak – Holy Spirit – Jesus – Moses – Muhammad – New Testament – Paul – Prophet – Sacrament – Sannyasin – Virgin Mary

To Talk About

Do you believe that miracles happen today? Describe any event that you have heard about or experienced that you would call a miracle.

Work

1. Name some of the experiences through which people can worship God.
2. Describe *two* religious experiences in the religions that you have studied.
3. What does it mean to be 'converted'?
4. How might a person experience a religious miracle?
5. How might a person experience God through prayer and worship?

B.4 BUDDHISM, CHRISTIANITY, HINDUISM

KEY QUESTION How do religious people picture God?

People have pictured God in two very different ways, although they often use both of them to give a full picture.

Two pictures of God

People speak of God as being:

- **transcendant.** This means that God is beyond the reach of all human understanding. In Extract A you can see an example of this taken from the Christian/Jewish scriptures. Several different ideas are included in the idea of God being transcendent:
  - God is eternal – without beginning or end. This means that God is outside and beyond time.
  - God is omnipotent – has unlimited power.
  - God is omniscient – knows everything and everyone.
  - God is omnipresent – found everywhere.
- **immanent.** Although God is omnipotent, He is also within the reach of human beings. This is when we think of God as personal and acting within human history. In the Jewish scriptures, for instance, God was deeply involved in the history of the Jews while, in the Christian scriptures, God shows that He is deeply concerned about human destiny through the coming of Jesus into the world.

> **EXTRACT A**
> "In the year that King Uzziah died, I saw the Lord. He was sitting on his throne, high and exalted, and his robe filled the whole Temple."
> [Isaiah 6.1]

Buddhists and God

Buddhism is different to the other major world religions. It does not believe in God. Instead, when a person becomes a Buddhist they commit themselves to having faith in:

- the Buddha himself.
- the dharma – the teachings of the Buddha.
- the sangha – the community of monks which is the custodian of the Buddha's teachings and the holy books.

Together, these are known as the Three Refuges. Some Buddhists do give 'god-like' qualities to the **Bodhisattvas**, Buddhists who have attained enlightenment and who stay behind on earth to help others to reach the enlightened state. They even pray to them sometimes in the hope that they can imitate their compassion and love. Beyond this, however, Buddhists are not interested in whether or not God exists. They believe that the Buddha taught them how to answer such important questions as, 'Why do people suffer?' without referring to God.

Christianity and God

Christians believe that God created the world in the beginning and continues to be involved in the everyday lives of His followers. God sent Jesus into the world to save human beings from their sins. After Jesus left the earth, God sent His Holy Spirit to guide His followers into all truth and He continues to do this today. God the Father, God the Son and God the Holy Spirit form the Trinity but this does not mean that Christians believe in three Gods. They do not. There is only one God and He has revealed Himself to the world in three different forms or persons.

These Buddhist monks are concerned, as are all Buddhists, to discover how the teachings of the Buddha can be applied to the major problems of life such as suffering.

Hinduism and God

Most people think that Hindus believe in many gods because there are thought to be 330 million gods, most of which are represented by a **murti** or image. In fact, Hindus believe in the one Supreme Power, Brahman, who is found everywhere in the universe and in everything that exists. Underneath Brahman is the Trimurti of three gods – Brahma (the creator); Shiva (the destroyer) and Vishnu (the preserver). Sometimes the gods appear to have contradictory personalities or characters but Hindus believe that this is true to life itself.

EXTRACT B
"*I am the nucleus of every creature... for without Me nothing can exist... The Lord lives in the heart of every creature.*"

[Bhagavad Gita 10:39–41]

KEY WORDS
Bodhisattva – Brahma – Brahman – Buddha – Dharma – Holy Spirit – Jesus – Murti – Sangha – Shiva – Three Refuges – Trimurti – Trinity – Vishnu

TO TALK ABOUT
Do you share the teaching of Buddhism that there are far more important questions to concern oneself about than the existence of God? If so, what do you think those questions are?

Work

1. Explain, in a sentence, what you understand by:
    a) the transcendance of God.
    b) the eternity of God.
    c) the immanence of God.
    d) the omnipotence of God.
    e) the omniscience of God.

2. Explain what the religion that you have studied believes about God.

B.5 Islam, Judaism, Sikhism and God

KEY QUESTION What do Muslims, Jews and Sikhs believe about God?

As we have seen, Christianity and Hinduism are monotheistic religions, believing firmly in one God. To this list of monotheistic religions we can now add Islam, Judaism and Sikhism.

Everything that a Muslim believes about God is found in the Qur'an.

Islam and God

Muslims call God Allah. They believe that Allah created the world in the beginning and filled it with good things for human beings to enjoy. Allah also provided them with their holy book, the Qur'an. It is through studying its teachings, and appreciating the beauty of the world around them, that Muslims can come to know the one true God, Allah. Because no one can equal Allah, Muslims are strictly forbidden from making any image of God as well as of the Prophet Muhammad ﷺ or any human image. Ninety-nine different names are given to Allah in the Qur'an and between them they sum up the divine character.

Allah is the perfect, all-knowing, merciful and all-powerful judge. He is the one before whom every human being will stand on the Day of Judgement to account for the life that they have led. Allah will then condemn each one of them to a life in hell or welcome them into Paradise – the place where Allah dwells for evermore.

Judaism and God

Jews believe that their God is one; is the Creator of the universe; is eternal, beyond time and space; knows all things (omniscient) and is to be found everywhere (omnipresent); is the source of all life in the universe; actively intervenes in the daily life of his followers and makes heavy moral and spiritual demands on those who belong to the Jewish faith. The beliefs that Jews hold about God are found in the Shema, a statement about God from the Jewish scriptures (Extract A).

In each Jewish home, **mezuzahs** (a small leather or plastic case) are placed on the doorposts of most of the rooms and each one of them contains a copy of the Shema. As Jews come and go in the different rooms, so they kiss their fingers and touch the mezuzah to show that they recognise God's authority over those in the house.

EXTRACT A

"*Hear, O Israel! The Lord is our God, the Lord alone. You shall love the Lord your God with all your heart, and with all your soul and with all your might. Take to heart these instructions with which I charge you this day. You shall teach them thoroughly to your children... write them on the doorposts of your house and upon your gates.*"

[Deuteronomy 6.4–9]

Sikhism and God

One of the central statements of Sikh belief is in a short hymn called the Mool Mantra ('basic teaching'). This is found at the beginning of the Guru Granth Sahib and is repeated every day during morning prayer. The first words of the Mool Mantra are 'Ik oankar', meaning, 'There is only one God – Waheguru.' God is beyond the understanding of human beings. He cannot be described because human beings can only use language – and this will always be less than what God is. God is neither male nor female. God is the Creator who made the world for human beings to enjoy. God is everywhere and beyond everything.

However, God also created human beings and made them so that they would know the difference between right and wrong. Although people know this, they still have to choose the right path. God is present in everyone's soul but can only be seen by those who are blessed. God is personal and available to everyone – whatever their religion. Sikhs believe that they should keep the name of God in the forefront of their minds, which they do by constantly repeating the word Waheguru (Wonderful Lord) under their breath.

No single religion can claim to be the only way to God. The different religions are just pointing different ways to God. It is not important which religion a person follows. What is important is that they follow God's teachings so that they have a chance of achieving **mukti** – escape from rebirth.

The mezuzah in a Jewish home is a constant reminder of God's presence with the family.

TO TALK ABOUT

Do you share the Sikh belief that all religions point in the same direction – towards God?

Work

1. Make a list of the different things that Muslims believe about Allah.
2. a) What is the Shema?
   b) How do Jews show their respect for God?
3. a) What is the Mool Mantra?
   b) Why is this prayer important for all Sikhs?
   c) What does the Mool Mantra say about God?

Key Words

Allah – Guru Granth Sahib – Mezuzah – Muhammad ﷺ – Mukti – Mool Mantra – Prophet – Qur'an – Shema – Waheguru

B.6 THE PROBLEM OF SUFFERING

KEY QUESTION What serious problems does suffering present to the theist?

The problem of suffering is the greatest challenge that the theist, the believer in God, faces. This is one of the main reasons why most atheists find it impossible to believe in God and why most agnostics seriously doubt that God exists. The existence of suffering seems to call into question the belief of theists that God is omnipotent (all-powerful); benevolent (all-good and loving); and omniscient (all-knowing).

Examples of suffering

It is often asked, 'How can there be a God?' after suffering touches the lives both of those we know and those who are strangers to us. There are many examples of suffering that seem to call into question the existence of an all-powerful God who has the interests of each one of us at heart:

- Natural disasters – floods, earthquakes, volcanoes and so on. These natural disasters kill thousands of people each year. The case of the tsunami disaster, which hit several countries on Boxing Day 2004, touched the whole world and caused it to ask many questions. The human race has little, if any, control over these disasters, although they can sometimes be caused by our inteference with the climate.
- Adults and children dying each year from hunger and malnutrition simply because they are unfortunate enough to have been born in the wrong place. Malnutrition is directly responsible for 20 million deaths each year, 25% (5 million) of which are of children under the age of 5.
- Children who are born with incurable illnesses or massive handicaps through no fault of their own or of their parents.
- Illnesses or accidents which rob loving families of parents or children.

It is not just the 'fact' of suffering that causes problems. It is also the 'unfairness' of it all. Some people go through life from birth to death with little experience of suffering, while others have to grapple with a disability or an illness from the moment they are born. One cannot help wondering whether there is an overall purpose behind life or not. The theist cannot escape the issue. In the end it all boils down to a simple dilemma:

Either: God wants to remove suffering but he cannot – in which case he is not all-powerful.

Or: God can remove suffering but does not – in which case he cannot be all-loving.

Everyone who believes in God has to live with this dilemma.

KEY WORDS

Agnostic – Atheist – Iblis – Jesus – Satan – Theist

Religion and suffering

No answer to the problem of suffering can be totally satisfactory. Three answers, however, are supplied by the world's religions:

1. Suffering is the direct result of a person's sinful actions. This was the answer given in the time of Jesus – and one that, to some extent, he shared. In some instances it seems to be true. A sufferer from lung cancer, for example, may be suffering as a direct result of years of smoking. How, though, can the child who contracts the HIV virus from his mother and dies before reaching his tenth birthday be blamed?

2. Suffering comes from an evil power that is opposed to God. This is the explanation favoured by Christianity, Islam and Judaism. Jews and Christians call this evil force **Satan** while Muslims call it **Iblis**. Thoughtful people wonder, however, who created this evil force? If it was God, why did he do it? If it was not God, who did?

3. God alone knows the meaning of suffering. The most well-known book about suffering is found in the Jewish scriptures – the book of Job. In the story, Job was a righteous man whose faith in God was tested when Satan was allowed by God to rob him of everything – his health, his family and his wealth. Job's final answer is that suffering is a mystery and to question God about it shows a lack of faith. Are thinking people, however, satisfied with this?

▲ This man has been blind since birth. It must raise questions in his mind about the fairness of life – and God.

Work

1. a) Describe *three* different kinds of suffering.
   b) How do you think that each kind of suffering you described in a) presents a challenge to the theist?

2. What are *three* of the explanations for suffering put forward by the different world religions?

3. "Suffering makes it impossible for a thoughtful person to believe in God." Do you agree with this statement? Give reasons for your opinion, showing that you have considered more than one point of view.

EXAM TIPS

There are several subjects in this course about which you will be expected to have formed some conclusions of your own – suffering is one of them. Whenever you are passing a personal opinion, you must be able to bring forward some arguments to support it. An unsupported opinion means no marks!

B.7 Two Questions about Suffering

KEY QUESTIONS What possible purpose could suffering serve?

There are two very important questions which go to the heart of the teaching of the different world religions on suffering:

Where does suffering come from?

Everyone who looks at the breadth and extent of suffering in the modern world begins to ask questions:

- Where did suffering come from in the first place and where does it come from today?
- Are human beings to blame for the suffering that affects them?
- Can we hold God responsible for the suffering in the world?
- Is there a powerful force of evil which causes the suffering in the world as part of its eternal battle against the power of good in the world – God?

The different world religions supply us with two very different answers to these questions:

1. Buddhists, Hindus and Sikhs believe in reincarnation. They teach that we all pass through many successive rebirths and that we carry forward from one life to the next the effects, good and bad, of our past actions. This is called the law of karma. If we live good lives, then we will return with a good rebirth. If, however, we live bad lives, then we will carry forward bad karma – and that could result in us suffering in the next life.
2. Christians, Jews and Muslims all teach that God has given to human beings the freedom to choose how they will live. This is called 'free will'. We can choose to live good, caring, thoughtful and God-respecting lives or we can live evil, selfish and thoughtless lives in which we exploit other people for our own ends. If we choose to live bad lives, then we cannot complain if we suffer as a result.

Both of these approaches arrive at the same conclusion – if we suffer, it is our own fault. We cannot blame anyone else but ourselves. We certainly cannot blame God.

What is the purpose of suffering?

It is not easy to find a purpose in most suffering. It seems to serve no useful purpose when we look at the suffering of innocent children or of families who have lost loved-ones in some natural disaster. Religious believers, however, might find some purpose behind much, if not all, of the suffering in the world. They would point to the fact that:

- pain sometimes tells us that something is seriously wrong with our body – and we can then do something about it. Toothache, for example, is usually an indication that a tooth requires attention.

For many people, the tsunami disaster on Boxing Day 2004 presented the greatest possible challenge to religious faith – what possible purpose could it serve?

EXTRACT A

"*Not to have known suffering is not to be truly human.*"

[A Jewish saying]

- some people claim that their suffering has made them better and more caring people. They have had to dig deep to find the courage or determination necessary to cope with their suffering and it has made them more aware of the suffering of others.
- some people discover that God is trying to teach them an important lesson through their suffering. When we are healthy, we tend to ignore the fact that we will all die. Suffering reminds us that we are all mortal, liable to death, and this may encourage us to change our priorities in life. It might show us that some things are much more important than making money, building up a business or simply enjoying ourselves.
- suffering helps us to stop taking everything in our life for granted. When things are going well all the time, we are inclined to forget that life is made up of bad as well as good times. It is good for us to be reminded of this sometimes.
- suffering can test our faith in God. We might say that we believe in a good or loving God and it is easy to believe that when all is going well. Can we say it, however, when things go wrong? Suffering can cause people to lose their faith in God. It can also strengthen that faith when it is under pressure. People might turn to their religion through prayer and worship and find their faith stronger as a result.

KEY WORDS

Karma – Reincarnation

Work

1. Explain how the world religions differ in the way that they explain suffering – and how they also agree.
2. What are the suggested purposes of suffering put forward by the different world religions?
3. Bring forward reasons why suffering might be thought of as a positive, rather than a negative, part of life.

TO TALK ABOUT

Do you think that trying to understand suffering in the world is more of a challenge to those who believe in God than it is to those who do not? Explain your answer.

B.8 Buddhism, Christianity, Hinduism

KEY QUESTION What is the teaching of Buddhism, Christianity and Hinduism about suffering?

Buddhism and suffering

The most important teaching in Buddhism is found in the Four Noble Truths. The first of these Truths is Dukkha – 'unsatisfactoriness', something which is not perfect or complete. The Buddha believed that every one of us suffers from a kind of illness. Everyone's life is made up of unsatisfactoriness or suffering. There are three kinds of dukkha:

1. Suffering – headaches, bereavements, etc. A mother giving birth suffers pain because the process is painful. A mother might also be worried that her baby will be born deformed and this causes her pain. Everyone knows that growing old is painful.
2. There are many pleasures in life but they are all unsatisfactory in the end because pleasures do not last.
3. Ordinary life itself is unsatisfactory until one becomes enlightened.

▲ Christians believe that the death of Jesus on the cross helps them to understand their own suffering.

This suffering stems from the selfishness, greed and craving that human beings have. Only when these cravings have been removed can inner satisfaction be found. The way to find such inner satisfaction is by following the Eightfold Path (the Middle Way). By following this way fully, a person can escape their cravings and sufferings and so reach enlightenment (nibbana).

Buddhism teaches that understanding and overcoming suffering is the most important lesson to learn in life.

Christianity and suffering

At the heart of the Christian faith is the story of Jesus, the Son of God, who lived a genuinely human and perfect life before dying on a cross. Jesus suffered a great deal because his death was necessary before God could forgive the sins of the human race. This is why Christians find in Jesus a Saviour who can understand, and share in, their suffering. Because Jesus rose from the dead after three days, Christians also look forward to the time when sickness and suffering will no longer exist – in heaven (Extract A).

AND SUFFERING

Christians pray that God might be with those who suffer and heal them. Christians have always been in the forefront of those seeking to bring comfort and healing to those who suffer in hospitals and hospices. Anointing the sick with oil is one of the sacraments carried out by the Roman Catholic Church. Christianity accepts the teaching of Judaism that all sickness and evil comes from the Prince of Darkness – Satan. It also suggests that suffering is the result of a person's sins.

> **EXTRACT A**
> "… [In heaven] God's home is with human beings! He will live with them… and He will be their God. God Himself will be with them, and He will be their God. He will wipe away all tears from their eyes. There will be no more death, no more grief or crying or pain. The old things have disappeared."
> [Revelation 21.3–4]

Hinduism and suffering

Hinduism recognises two kinds of evil:

1. Natural evil. Samsara (the cycle of birth, death and rebirth) is a natural evil because the individual life-force, or atman, has to go through birth and rebirth many times. Suffering is part of samsara.
2. Moral evil. Hindus believe that we have a human tendency to commit such moral evils as theft, adultery, incest, lying and murder.

Moral evil is explained by the law of karma. All suffering comes from human actions. If a person experiences suffering in this world, it is because of bad karma from a previous life. Suffering is not the fault of God or anyone else. It is our own fault (see Extract B).

> **EXTRACT B**
> "Great souls who have become one with Me [Brahman] have reached the highest goal. They do not undergo re-birth, a condition which is impermanent and full of pain and suffering."
> [The Bhagavad Gita 8.15]

KEY WORDS

Atman – Buddha – Dukkha – Eightfold Path – Four Noble Truths – Jesus – Karma – Middle Way – Nibbana – Roman Catholic Church – Sacrament – Samsara – Satan

TO TALK ABOUT

How do you think that having the cross as the central symbol of Christianity might help people to find meaning in their own experiences of suffering?

Work

1. a) How does Christianity explain the existence of suffering?
   b) How does Christianity suggest that a person can find comfort in their suffering?
2. How would a Buddhist explain the existence of suffering in the world?
3. What explanation would a Hindu put forward to explain suffering?

B.9 Islam, Judaism, Sikhism and

Islam and suffering

KEY QUESTION
What is the teaching of Islam, Judaism and Sikhism on suffering?

Muslims believe that nothing can happen to them which is not permitted by Allah. Nothing happens in the world unless Allah wills it. Suffering and pain are part of Allah's plan. Suffering is a test of faith that is set by Allah (Extract A). When God created the world, He appointed **Adam** to look after it as his Vice-regent. Human beings were made superior to the angels because they were given the precious gift of free will.

The angels were commanded to bow down to humans and respect their superiority but Iblis refused to do so. As a result, Iblis was given the kingdom of hell as his dominion and told to test the faith of the people in Allah. Evil and suffering are the ways that he has at his disposal to do this.

EXTRACT A
"We shall test your steadfastness with fear and famine, with loss of property and life and crops. Give good news to those who endure with fortitude; who in adversity say: 'We belong to God and to Him we shall return.' On such men will be God's blessing and mercy; such men are rightly guided."

[The Qur'an 2.155–156]

Judaism and suffering

Jews ask the usual questions about suffering and God but there is one extra important Jewish question: 'Why did God allow six million Jews to be put to death in the German concentration camps of the Second World War?' This event, called the **Holocaust**, puts a whole new perspective on suffering. It led to many Jews:

- losing their faith in God altogether because they blamed God for what happened to their fellow Jews.
- coming to the conclusion that, at best, they are worshipping a God who has only limited powers.
- believing that this was the ultimate test of their faith in God.
- deciding to continue as before, believing that, while they could not understand what had happened to them, they must keep on having faith in God.

The Jewish scriptures contain many accounts and stories of people suffering. Underlying all of these accounts is the belief that suffering is, in the end, for the benefit of the person concerned. Suffering is a fact of life. It comes from God and so there has to be a positive side to it. People who suffer need to draw on an inner strength that they did not know they had – and this means they emerge as better people at the end.

SUFFERING

The Yad Veshem memorial was erected to commemorate those Jews who died in the Holocaust.

Sikhism and suffering

Guru Nanak taught that suffering is caused by wrong attachment, treating natural relationships as if they are going to last forever. Only one form of relationship truly lasts forever, is eternal, and that is between God and the worshipper. Physical pain can be a good thing if it disillusions those who are self-satisfied. As the Adi Granth says: "Pain is the remedy and pleasure the sickness; where there is nothing but pleasure there is no yearning for God" (469). By doing good things, a person can make sure that they will return in the next life without the suffering. They can rise above this by being kind and doing good deeds.

KEY WORDS

Adam – Adi Granth – Allah – Guru Nanak – Holocaust – Iblis

TO TALK ABOUT

How do the religions that you have studied suggest that suffering might be a positive thing? Do you agree with them? Give your reasons one way or the other.

Work

1. a) How do Muslims understand suffering?

   b) Who is Iblis and what part does he play in a Muslim's experience of suffering?

2. a) What was the Holocaust?

   b) What have been the different responses of Jews to the Holocaust?

3. How does a Sikh explain suffering?

B.10 Life after death

> **KEY QUESTION**   Is there any evidence for life after death?

What happens to each one of us after we die? Does the body slowly disintegrate in the grave until all traces of it disappears? Is there, as many believe, a part that survives beyond death and, if so, in what form? Do we just survive after death in the memories of those we have left behind? A belief in some form of survival after death is almost as old as humankind itself.

A life after death?

Is there any strong reason for thinking that people survive beyond death? There is certainly no strong evidence, but three non-religious reasons have been put forward:

1 **Ghosts and spiritism.** Many people believe that they have seen a ghost, although no one is sure just what they could be if they exist. Some people think that ghosts are the spirits of dead people who haven't yet managed to gain admittance to the afterlife, but that is pure guess-work. Most people who claim to have seen a ghost describe it as an apparition in some recognisable form. These apparitions do not seem to obey the normal rules of existence. They seem to be attracted to particular locations – mainly old houses – which may be empty or occupied. Sometimes, people become so aware of their presence that they employ an exorcist to expel them because their presence makes them feel uncomfortable.

Spiritism is a religious movement that is loosely attached to the Christian religion, in which people known as mediums claim to be able to contact the spirits of people who have died. Relatives are invited to listen to messages from 'the other side' transmitted through the medium – these are called 'seances'. The medium acts as a 'channel' for these messages. The messages, however, are couched in such general terms that they could easily be forgeries – and many of them plainly are. A major problem is that some people are so desperate to contact their dead loved ones that they are very vulnerable and open to the suggestions of others.

2 **Near-death experiences.** It is claimed that such experiences take place when a person is close to death without actually dying. This might happen during a serious surgical operation. Having recovered, the person then describes their experience as being conscious of leaving their body behind and looking down on it from above. Some have said that they felt drawn towards a bright light or met people who they recognised. People from very different backgrounds and religions claim to have had near-death experiences.

It is not easy to know just what to make of these claims. It seems that something happens to the functioning of the brain as death approaches in everyone, but most people cannot report on this because they die. Perhaps the brain begins to slow down for a short time before it closes down altogether at death. It may be that the oxygen supply to the brain begins to be shut off and this produces some extraordinary sensations. This induces images which, when people wake up, suggest to them that they have been in contact with the afterlife.

3 **Visits from dead relatives**. Some people believe that they have been visited by the spirits of dead relatives who assure them that they are well and happy in the afterlife. Sometimes the visitation is to inform the person of a coming event and sometimes it is simply to offer them some form of reassurance.

How important are these so-called evidences of a life after death? It must be said that every so-called event in this area is open to considerable doubt. Nothing can be proved. There is no clear evidence that ghosts appear; that people have 'near-death' experiences; that mediums can contact the dead; or that relatives ever appear to those they have left behind. Most of it is undoubtedly wishful thinking. If someone believes in life after death, it will almost certainly be because of their religious beliefs and not because of any experience that they have had.

Some people claim to have seen a ghost, but the evidence for such appearances is very uncertain.

Work

1. Write short notes on:
   a) ghosts.
   b) spiritism.
   c) 'near-death' experiences.
2. Why do you think that someone today might believe in a life after death?

TO TALK ABOUT

Do you believe in a life after death? Can you understand and appreciate the arguments put forward by those who hold the opposing point of view to your own?

B.11 Buddhism, Christianity, Hinduism

KEY QUESTION What are the teachings of Buddhism, Christianity and Hinduism about life after death?

All of the religions studied in this book believe in life after death. These beliefs can be divided into two different types:

1 **A belief in resurrection** (coming back to life). Christianity, Islam and Judaism all teach that each person has just one life which is ended by death. At some future time, their soul and/or their body is brought back to life and lives forever in heaven or hell.

2 **A belief in reincarnation.** Hindus, Buddhists and Sikhs believe that the soul or spirit does not die at death but passes into another body. The way that a person lives affects the level at which their soul returns. Eventually, the soul reaches paradise and rebirth stops.

In India, Hindus cremate their dead as close to the River Ganges as possible. The ashes are scattered on the waters and those alive hope that the deceased will escape rebirth.

In this topic we are going to look at three religions – Buddhism, Christianity and Hinduism – and the beliefs that each religion holds about life after death.

Buddhism and life after death

The Buddha taught that a person can break the effect of their karma by giving up their cravings and break the samsara reincarnation cycle by seeking nibbana. A person must stop the succession of rebirths on their own. One can become an **arhat** (enlightened person) and reach nibbana by following the teachings of the Buddha. Nibbana is absolute truth, spiritual freedom, freedom from space and time, from illusion, from passion and from all the passing things of this world. It is a state of nothingness. It was the Buddha who said: "Nibbana is made of nothing at all."

EXTRACT A
"To realise that life ends in death is to escape from the control of death."
[The Buddha]

KEY WORDS

Arhat – Buddha – Jesus – Karma – Moksha – Nibbana – Parable – Reincarnation – Resurrection – Samsara – Yoga

AND LIFE AFTER DEATH

Christianity and life after death

Christianity teaches that there is a heaven and there is a hell. When the soul of a believer dies, it goes straight to heaven where it dwells with God for eternity. Heaven is the reward at the end for those who have served God faithfully. In his parable of the Sheep and Goats (Matthew 25.31–36), Jesus said that it is those who care for the needy and feed the hungry while they are alive who will enter God's kingdom – heaven. This is why Jesus told his followers to store up spiritual treasure in heaven and not to spend their time concerning themselves with acquiring material wealth.

Christians believe that the Resurrection of Jesus from the dead is the guarantee that they, too, will be raised from the dead on the Day of Judgement. They also believe that their soul is immortal and will be reunited with the body as the good are sent to heaven and the wicked to hell. Christians disagree about whether hell is a place of everlasting torment or not, but few, nowadays, believe that it is.

Hinduism and life after death

Hindus believe in reincarnation. This means that they believe in the law of karma which governs each rebirth and reflects the life that someone has led in their last life. They try to achieve good karma by following the path of yoga (meditation). Hindus believe that they can improve their chances of rebirth at a higher level by:

- worshipping the deities.
- living a good life.
- reading the holy books and following their teachings.
- going on pilgrimages to holy places.
- performing good deeds and living a good life.

The intention of each life is to reach moksha and so escape from the cycle of birth, death and rebirth.

EXTRACT B
"When all desires which shelter in the heart detach themselves, then does a mortal man become immortal: to Brahman [the Supreme Spirit] he wins through."

[Brihadaranyaka Upanishad]

TO TALK ABOUT
We have seen how the major world religions believe in either resurrection or reincarnation. Which of these two beliefs about life after death do you favour, and why?

Work

1. What are the *two* basic types of belief about life after death and which religions fit into each group?
2. What is nibbana and what do Buddhists believe about it?
3. What does Christianity teach about the fate of people after death?

B.12 Islam, Judaism, Sikhism and life

KEY QUESTION What are the teachings of Islam, Judaism and Sikhism about life after death?

Islam and life after death

Muslims believe that death is only the end of the present life, since there is a life beyond this which never ends (Akhirah). Allah is the God of the Day of Judgement. This is proclaimed in very graphic terms in the Qur'an (see Extract A).

> **EXTRACT A**
> "When the sun shall be folded up, and the stars shall fall, and when the mountains shall be set in motion… and the seas shall boil… then shall every soul know what it hath done."
> [Surah 81]

This turmoil will begin suddenly when angels sound the trumpet once; at the second blast, all living creatures will die and, at the third, all will rise from death and await God's judgement. Then all will pass over the abyss of hell by the As-Sirat Bridge, which is "finer than a hair and sharper than a sword's edge". The righteous will cross into Paradise while the wicked will fall into hell. Those who pass into Paradise will find places reserved for them in mansions where they will be waited on by servants. The most important thing is that they will spend eternity in the presence of Allah.

Judaism and life after death

Jews believe that the soul is immortal but they do not have very clear teachings about life after death. There is a reference in the Jewish scriptures to **Sheol**, a shadowy underground place where the ghosts of the dead go while waiting for the resurrection of the body. It is said to be divided up into sections to receive the good and the bad. Today, strict Orthodox Jews look forward to the coming of the Messiah who will:

- set up his kingdom of justice on earth after a series of disasters and terrors.
- overcome Israel's enemies and judge all people.
- bring the dead back to life to await God's kingdom.

Liberal and Reform Jews, however, do not expect the Messiah to come. Instead, they look forward to an age of kindness and justice which will be the time of judgement. Everyone, Jew and non-Jew, will receive the rewards of living a good life.

> **KEY WORDS**
>
> Allah – Messiah – Qur'an – Reincarnation – Resurrection – Sheol

> **TO TALK ABOUT**
>
> Do you think that this life is simply a preparation for eternity or an end to be enjoyed in itself?

AFTER DEATH

Muslims believe that hell is a place of eternal torment and punishment.

Sikhism and life after death

Sikhs believe that each person is made up of a body and soul. The body belongs to the physical universe in which it is born, lives and dies. The soul, however, belongs to the spiritual universe which is God. A person is reincarnated time and time again until they are eventually united with God. The soul is a minute part of the Eternal Soul, God, and has existed since the time of creation and it remains separate from God until it is reabsorbed back into Him. The soul passes through all levels, called the evolution of the soul, until it reaches the highest form – the human one (see Extract B).

A person's deeds follow their soul like a shadow. It is their good deeds, and the grace of God, which enable a Sikh to be reunited with God. It is by repentance, prayer and love that they can earn God's grace. The fate of the wicked, though, is endless reincarnation until they finally repent and deserve God's grace.

> **EXTRACT B**
> "For several births I was a worm… an elephant, a fish, a deer… a bird, a serpent… a bull, a horse. After a long period of time has the human frame come into being. Seek now union with the Lord of the Universe, for now is the time."
>
> [Guru Granth Sahib 176]

EXAM TIPS
It is important to be able to distinguish between the different religions that believe in resurrection or reincarnation. Make sure that you understand what it is that makes the belief of your chosen religion distinctive.

Work

1. Describe what Muslims believe about life after death.
2. Who is the Messiah and what do many Jews believe he will do when he comes?
3. What do Sikhs believe about the soul and the body?

87

B.13 LIFE AFTER DEATH AND LIVING TODAY

KEY QUESTION What do the different religions teach about the link between this life and the next?

All religions teach that there is a very close link between the way that people live their lives on earth and what happens to them after death. There are two ways in which this belief is expressed:

1. **A belief in karma.** Buddhists, Hindus and Sikhs believe in karma – that their actions in this life affect the form in which they return in the next. This is often expressed in the statement: 'What a man sows so shall he reap.' Everything that a person does, in thought and deed, will affect their next rebirth. Bad or negative karma is the result of bad and evil thoughts and actions. Good or positive karma is the result of good deeds and thoughts. It is only through acquiring good karma that a person can hope to escape the cycle of birth, death and rebirth.

2. **A belief in the Day of Judgement.** Christianity, Judaism and Islam teach that everyone will be held accountable for the way that they have lived in their one life (Extract A). Each religion has its own way of judging what is a 'good life'. For Muslims, for instance, it is to follow the teachings of the Qur'an, to pray, to fast, to go on pilgrimage and to perform good deeds.

> **EXTRACT A**
> "And I saw the dead, great and small alike, standing before the throne. Books were opened, and then another book was opened, the book of the living."
> [Revelation 20.12]

The teaching of Buddhism

Every Buddhist hopes to move closer towards nibbana by: reading their Holy scriptures; faithfully following the teachings of the Buddha; meditating; following the Eightfold Path (the Middle Way); and showing loving kindness to all creatures – animal and human.

The teaching of Christianity

When Jesus was asked which were the two most important of the commandments, he replied that it was to love God and to love one's neighbour. He implied that those who wished to enter heaven needed to obey these two commandments. They would express their faith through meeting with other Christians, reading the Bible, praying and putting their faith into practice by helping the poor and the needy.

The teaching of Hinduism

Most Hindus believe that they can achieve a better rebirth by following meditation (yoga) and reading their holy books. They must also offer the appropriate worship and offerings to their family deity (god). This will build up good karma for them and so improve their chances of enjoying a good rebirth. The aim of all Hindus is to reach moksha, after many rebirths, and so be joined to Brahman and escape the cycle of rebirth.

Members of all religions believe that there is a direct link between the way that they live today and what happens to them after death. ▶

The teaching of Judaism

As we have seen in Topic B.12 there is little clear teaching about life after death in Judaism. Jews believe that what matters is how people live here and now. They do hope for some form of eternal life and personal immortality and there is a need to live one's life in the light of this. Jews believe in heaven and hell but do not share the Muslim belief that hell is a place of eternal punishment and torment. They cannot believe that a gracious God could ever wish this on His creation. Instead, in hell, the wicked are cleansed from their sins before they are made fit to enter heaven. This belief is similar to the Roman Catholic belief in **purgatory**.

The teaching of Sikhism

Like Hindus, Sikhs also believe that their great goal in life is to free themselves from the cycle of birth, death and rebirth (mukti). They are helped to reach this goal if they read the Guru Granth Sahib; worship in the gurdwara; say their prayers; and carry out good deeds. You can read what Guru Nanak had to say about the link between the worship of God and the carrying out of worldly tasks in Extract B. This is why meditation plays such an important part in the everyday life of a Sikh – it is the best way of keeping God at the forefront of one's mind.

EXTRACT B
"*Do your daily duties with hands and feet, but concentrate on the Lord.*"

[Guru Nanak]

KEY WORDS

Bible – Brahman – Buddha – Eightfold Path – Gurdwara – Guru Granth Sahib – Guru Nanak – Jesus – Karma – Middle Way – Moksha – Mukti – Nibbana – Purgatory – Qur'an – Roman Catholic Church – Yoga

TO TALK ABOUT

Which of the two – reincarnation or resurrection – strikes you as being the most likely explanation for life after death? Try to give as many reasons as you can for the choice you have made.

Work

1. What is the suggested link in the religions you have studied between believing in an afterlife and living the present life?
2. What are those people who believe in karma trying to achieve through the way that they live their present lives?
3. How do you think that believing in a coming Day of Judgement might have an effect on the way that someone lives?

Exam questions

Question 1 – The existence of God
1. What is:
   a) an atheist?
   b) an agnostic?
   c) a theist?
2. How might religious experience, their own or that of others, help some people to believe in God?
3. What do you think are the main reasons why many people find it impossible to believe in God?

Question 2 – Suffering
1. You believe in God and belong to a worshipping community. How do you think that the presence of undeserved suffering in the world would affect, or even destroy, your faith in God?
2. How does the religion(s) you have studied explain the existence of suffering in the world?
3. "Nearly all the suffering in the world is the result of human sin or misbehaviour." Do you agree with this statement? Give reasons for your answer, showing that you have considered more than one point of view.

Question 3 – Life after death
1. What is nibbana and how do Buddhists hope to reach it?
2. Explain the beliefs that the religion(s) you have studied holds about life after death.
3. What are the *two* broad beliefs held by the different religions about life after death?

Question 4 – The existence of God
1. What is the Cosmological argument for the existence of God? Is it a convincing argument?
2. Imagine that a group of believers from all the different religions come together. What arguments might they put forward for believing in the existence of God?
3. "The world shows clear evidence of being designed so it must have been created by God." Do you agree with this statement? Give reasons for your answer, showing that you have considered more than one point of view.

Question 5 – Suffering
1. Describe, and give examples of, the different kinds of suffering in the world.
2. How do you think religious people would explain the existence and the unfairness of suffering in the world? Do you find their explanations convincing?
3. "Surely if an all-powerful and all-loving God existed, there would be no suffering." Do you agree with this statement? Give reasons for your answer, showing that you have considered more than one point of view.

Question 6 – Life after death
1. Write *four* sentences about each of the following:
   a) Resurrection.
   b) Reincarnation.
2. What do the following people expect to happen to them when they die?
   a) Muslims.
   b) Jews.
   c) Sikhs.
3. "You need to believe in God to believe in a life after death." Do you agree with this statement? Give reasons for your answer, showing that you have considered more than one point of view.

SECTION C LIFE ISSUES

In this section you will find out about:

C.1 The sanctity of life
C.2 The facts about abortion
C.3 The responses of the different religions to abortion
C.4 The pro-life and the pro-choice approaches to abortion
C.5 The real cost of going to war
C.6 The Just War theory
C.7 The Holy War and pacifism
C.8 Prejudice and discrimination
C.9 Racism
C.10 Sexism
C.11 Other forms of prejudice
C.12 The attitude of the world religions to prejudice

C.1 THE SANCTITY OF LIFE

KEY QUESTION What do people mean when they speak of the 'sanctity of life'?

We all have many important moral decisions to make as we move through life from birth to death. Some decisions will be straightforward, while others will be very complicated. As we make these decisions, we will need to take different things into consideration:

- our own needs and wants.
- the needs and wants of other people who will be directly or indirectly affected by our decision.
- our ideas and beliefs about what is the right and wrong thing to do.
- any religious beliefs that we hold and the teachings from its holy books and other places.

Most moral decisions are very complicated and a final decision is rarely reached easily.

▲ Many religions, including Christianity and Islam, do not believe that homosexuality is an acceptable part of life.

Three life issues

The specification asks you to look at three different life issues. It is perfectly possible, although unlikely, that you will never have to face up to the challenge that these issues present. It is more likely that they will touch your life, directly or indirectly, at some time in the future. These issues are:

- **Abortion.** This is the decision that a pregnant girl or woman has to make if she wants to bring a pregnancy to an end. By its very nature this is a decision that raises all kinds of issues. Because it is a very personal decision, a person may find it very difficult to seek help and guidance from someone else.
- **War and peace.** Hopefully, you will never have to decide whether to fight and risk your life to defend your country. It is a decision, however, that many of your grandparents, parents, aunts and uncles have faced in the not too distant past. Would you be a pacifist and a conscientious objector, or would you fight? How would you decide?

- **Prejudice.** Prejudice is an attitude of mind that considers one group of people, who are in some way distinctive, inferior to others. It may be because they are black, disabled, male or female, Jewish or gay. When prejudice translates itself into action, it becomes discrimination.

As we will see, the six world religions have different approaches to many of these issues, although they do agree about the importance of the sanctity of all life (see Extract A).

> **EXTRACT A**
> "*God alone is the lord of life from its beginning to its end: no one can, under any circumstances, claim for himself directly to destroy an innocent human being.*"
> [The Catechism of the Catholic Church 2258]

The sanctity of life

Most religious people believe that life is a gift from God and so is sacred. Considering life to be sacred means that it is to be treated as holy and, therefore, to be valued and preserved. This is a very important teaching in Christianity, Judaism and Islam. It has very clear implications for two of the life issues that we are looking at:

- **Abortion.** Without exception, the different Christian Churches are opposed to abortion – with the Roman Catholic Church being the most outspoken in its condemnation. This Church teaches that a foetus has life from the moment that it is conceived in the womb, and so any deliberate attempt to remove it is murder. The other religions mainly agree that abortion is wrong, although most allow it if the life of the mother is at risk.
- **War.** War, inevitably, involves the taking of life. This is what those who fight in a war are trained to do. Here, the position is complicated, however, because Islam has a concept of a Holy War (a **jihad**), while Christians and Jews have fought what have been called Holy Wars or Just Wars in the past.

KEY WORDS

Abortion – Jihad – Just War – Roman Catholic Church

TO TALK ABOUT

Imagine that you are facing one of the life issues covered in this section. How would you begin to decide what to do? Where would you go for advice? Would you seek any guidance from religion or religious people?

Work

1. How do most of us make moral decisions?
2. a) What do you understand by the phrase: 'the sanctity of life'?
   b) Do you think that believing all forms of life are sacred is a helpful principle to follow?

C.2 Abortion – the facts

> **KEY QUESTION** When is an abortion in the United Kingdom legal?

The word '**abortion**' can be used correctly to refer to:

- the deliberate removal of a growing foetus from a woman's womb using a surgical procedure. This is the sense in which we will be using the word.
- a miscarriage ('spontaneous abortion') in which a foetus is expelled naturally from the womb. About 30% of all pregnancies end in this way, usually within the first 12 weeks of pregnancy and, often, without the woman being aware of it.

Abortion – the law

Before 1967, all abortions in England and Wales were illegal. Women who wanted an abortion were forced to visit untrained 'back-street' abortionists and this put their life seriously at risk. Each year, about 60 women died as a result of an illegal abortion which involved a combination of whisky, hot baths and knitting needles! The 1967 Abortion Act was designed to put an end to this. It ruled that a woman could legally obtain an abortion if two doctors agreed that:

- the mother's life is at risk if the pregnancy is allowed to continue.
- there is a risk to the mother's mental or physical health if she is to give birth.
- there is a risk to the mental or physical health of existing children in the family if another baby is born.
- there is a substantial risk that the baby might be born with severe physical or mental abnormalities.

The law was amended in 1990 to prevent any abortions being performed after 24 weeks of pregnancy, unless the mother's life was at risk. This was because medical advances made it possible to keep a premature baby alive if it was born after 24 weeks of pregnancy.

When does life begin?

In any discussion of abortion, the most important question is: 'When does life actually begin?' There are three possible answers:

1 Life begins at the moment when the sperm fertilises the ovum (egg). This is the view held by Hindus, Sikhs, Jews and many Christians. Buddhists believe that life begins even earlier, since all human beings are involved in the almost endless cycle of samsara (birth, death and rebirth) and so their present existence is unlikely to be their first.

This woman is very excited about the birth of her baby. What kind of circumstances, however, might lead a woman to consider having an abortion?

2. Life begins at some point during pregnancy. Some religions teach that life begins when God implants a soul in the body – some would say this happens after 90 days of pregnancy but Muslims believe it happens after 120 days.

3. Life either begins when the baby can survive independently of its mother (called the time of 'viability') or at the moment when it is born.

Abortion – the facts

- Before 1967, at least 200,000 abortions were carried out illegally each year in this country. Many women died each year from their injuries, while thousands more were scarred for life or made infertile by botched 'back-street' abortions.
- During 1971, 104,000 abortions were carried out. By 1991, this figure had risen to 190,000. One in every 12 abortions is carried out on a woman who is more than 12 weeks pregnant. About 18% of all pregnancies (1 in 6) now end in an abortion.
- The largest increase in the number of abortions since 1968 has been in the 16–19 age group. One in every 40 women in this age group has an abortion every year.
- Most abortions are carried out because it is felt that the mental or physical health of the mother would be at risk if the pregnancy was allowed to continue.
- 20% of all abortions in England and Wales are performed on women who come from other countries – such as Spain and Eire – where abortion is illegal.

EXTRACT A

"*The child, by reason of its physical and mental immaturity, needs special safeguards and care, including appropriate legal protection, before as well as after birth.*"

[United Nations Declaration of Human Rights]

KEY WORDS

Abortion – Samsara

Work

Carry out a class brainstorming session. Come up with as many answers to these questions as you can:
a) What is the meaning and purpose of life? Why are we here?
b) When is abortion acceptable – if at all?
c) When is abortion unacceptable – if at all?

Bring together the answers of your class to see whether there is a general level of agreement.

TO TALK ABOUT

Do you agree with the United Nations Declaration of Human Rights that society has a responsibility to look after its most vulnerable groups? If so, what are the implications of this for abortion?

C.3 Abortion – The Religious Responses

KEY QUESTION What do the world religions teach about abortion?

The rights and wrongs of this life issue go to the very heart of religion – is all life sacred and, if so, must it be preserved at all costs? The six major world religions reach a fair measure of agreement on abortion.

Buddhism and abortion

Buddhism teaches that no living thing should be killed. As Extract A shows, this is the First Precept and so is fundamental to the Buddhist understanding of life. Abortion involves the taking of the life of a living being. It is accepted by many Buddhists, however, that there may be two exceptions to this – when the life of the mother is at risk and when the baby would be born with considerable abnormalities.

> **EXTRACT A**
> "*I will not harm any living thing.*"
> [First Precept]

Christianity and abortion

Abortion is a very serious issue for many Christians and one that brings about serious disagreements. The Roman Catholic Church teaches that it is very wrong to take human life at any time. It does not even accept that an abortion is justified if the life of the mother is at risk or if she has been raped. Other Churches, such as the Methodist Church, accept that there are circumstances which might justify an abortion – including a direct threat to the life of the mother and the probable birth of a severely handicapped child.

> **EXTRACT B**
> "*Surely you know that you are God's Temple and that God's Spirit lives in you! So if anyone destroys God's Temple, God will destroy him.*"
> [2 Corinthians 3.16–17]

Hinduism and abortion

Abortion is legal in India where over 80% of the population is Hindu. Hinduism, though, teaches that all life is sacred because all life is part of God. Since all life comes from God, so all life is special. Abortion results in bad karma. The amount of bad karma depends on the circumstances – it is small if the life of the mother has been saved through an abortion.

Islam and abortion

The Qur'an teaches that abortion is a sin against Allah – and so is forbidden. Many Muslims, though, allow an abortion if the mother's life is at risk. This is because the mother is alive and has great responsibilities, while the foetus only has a potential life. Otherwise, abortion is forbidden. The Qur'an reminds mothers that, on the Day of Judgement, aborted infants will want to know from their mothers why they were killed.

Judaism and abortion

Jews find abortion very objectionable. It destroys a life created by God (Extract C). It is acceptable, however, if the pregnancy has become dangerous for the mother. In this case, the earlier an abortion is carried out the better. The **Talmud**, an important holy book, teaches that the foetus does not become a human being until the 41st day of pregnancy.

> ### EXTRACT C
> "*You created every part of me; you put me together in my mother's womb.*"
>
> [Psalm 139.13]

Sikhism and abortion

Sikhism is strongly opposed to abortion. It teaches that while God, Nam, is invisible He can always be seen through the world of nature that He has created. That includes all life, especially human life. To destroy any part of that life is to destroy part of God's creation – and that is wrong.

▲ This sculpture perfectly captures the attitude of religion to abortion. Religion teaches that every baby, born and unborn, is in the safe keeping of God and must be treated as sacred.

KEY WORDS

Abortion – Allah – Karma – Methodist Church – Nam – Qur'an – Roman Catholic Church – Samsara – Talmud

TO TALK ABOUT

It is generally accepted by most religions that an abortion is justified if the life of the mother is at risk should the pregnancy continue. Is this a conclusion that you agree with? Explain your answer.

Work

1. a) Write down *two* pieces of information about the attitude of your chosen religions to abortion.
   b) What appear to be your chosen religions' key reasons for opposing abortion?
2. "Abortion is no more than a form of murder." Do you agree with this statement? Give reasons for your answer, showing that you have considered more than one point of view. In your answer, you should refer to *one* particular religion.

C.4 Abortion – the issues

KEY QUESTION What are the arguments for and against abortion?

Abortion is an issue that strongly divides people. Many believe that every woman has the right to decide what she does with her own body (pro-choice). Others believe that abortion is morally wrong whatever the circumstances (pro-life). The arguments put forward by both sides have to be seriously considered.

Arguments for abortion (pro-choice)

The main arguments in favour of giving a woman free choice whether to continue with a pregnancy or to have an abortion are:

1. Every woman has the right to do as she wishes with her own body. The foetus is part of her body until the moment when the baby is born.
2. Every baby has the right to be born into a family that can meet its basic needs for food, shelter and love. If those needs cannot be met, it might be more humane for the foetus to be aborted. It is a fact that single mothers are among the poorest members of society.
3. A mentally or physically handicapped child demands total dedication from its carers for the whole of its life. Many parents cannot provide this level of support and it is unfair to expect them to do so.
4. There are far too many unwanted babies in the world already. Unless a baby is really wanted, it is better for a woman to have an abortion.
5. Other members of the family also have their own rights and these must be respected. In large families, another child may be an intolerable burden for everyone to carry.
6. A woman who has been raped should not, under any circumstances, be compelled to give birth to her attacker's baby.

Abortion is never an easy option for a woman to take. It requires a sensible and mature decision. If the decision to go ahead with an abortion is taken, then a high emotional price will be paid – whatever the mother's situation. Every person should be allowed to make their own free decision without coming under any outside pressure.

Arguments against abortion (pro-life)

The main arguments against abortion are:

1. Abortion is murder – the killing of another human being. It is the killing of a human being who cannot defend itself in any way. Life begins the moment a baby is conceived in the womb.
2. The unborn child is genetically distinct from its mother from conception onwards, and so a mother does not have the right to kill her baby.

Protests against abortion are often violent – especially in the United States.

3   Abortion is destroying hundreds of thousands of human beings who might go on to achieve great things for humanity and live very useful lives.
4   Handicapped people are human beings. It is an insult to them to suggest that they should be destroyed before they are born simply because they are handicapped. Many of them go on to live happy and fulfilled lives, as well as giving great joy to those who look after them. Vulnerable people, such as the very young, have a right to expect protection from society.
5   A foetus is a human being from the moment it is conceived. It has the perfect right to life from this time onwards.
6   An abortion has a considerable effect on most women, often leaving them with feelings of guilt for a very long time and this shows that they have regretted what they have done.
7   It would be far better for someone who is pregnant, and does not want to keep the baby, to offer it up for adoption. There is a long line of couples who cannot have babies of their own waiting to adopt.

Work

1. What are the main arguments put forward by those who describe themselves as being pro-choice?
2. What are the main arguments put forward by those who describe themselves as being pro-life?
3. Do you think that a foetus has a 'right' to live?

TO TALK ABOUT

What are your own feelings about abortion? Are you swayed by any of these arguments for and against?

KEY WORD

Abortion

C.5 The cost of going to war

KEY QUESTION What are the different kinds of war?

War has always been a fact of life. There is little reason to hope that nations will find new and more peaceful ways of solving their conflicts and disagreements in the future. The period since the end of the Second World War, in 1945, has seen more conflicts than any other similar period in history.

Different kinds of war

Technically, a war is any armed conflict that lasts for longer than 60 minutes and in which regular armed forces are involved. During the 20th century, more than 100 million people died as a direct result of war:

- In the First World War, nine million people died and over 21 million were seriously injured. 95% of the casualties were soldiers.
- In the Second World War, there were 55 million deaths of which 16 million were soldiers and 39 million civilians.

These figures show a big change in the way that wars were fought as time went on. With modern weapons, the way that wars are now fought, over 90% of casualties are civilians. These conflicts fall into three groups:

1. Conflicts between nations – since 1945 there have been more than 300 armed conflicts.

2. Civil wars and 'wars of liberation' – when the two main tribes in Rwanda were involved in a civil war in the 1990s more than one million people from one tribe alone were slaughtered.

3. Wars against terrorism – the 21st century wars in Afghanistan and Iraq fit into this category. Wars to eradicate terrorists are unlike any other armed conflict and are rarely victorious.

EXTRACT A
"*Transgressors shall be utterly destroyed, the future of the wicked shall be cut off.*"
[The Jewish scriptures. Psalm 37.38–39]

TO TALK ABOUT
Why do you think that the refugee problem has been described as one of the greatest challenges facing the world today?

This graphically illustrates the price of war in terms of lives lost. ▶

The cost of war

The cost of going to war must be measured in terms of:

- **the destruction caused.** The number of people killed and injured; the destruction of towns, villages and countryside; and the number of families whose lives have been changed forever must all be taken into account. When the Allied Forces, led by the USA and Britain, undertook the Gulf War in 1991 against Iraq, the cost is believed to have been $71 billion but this did not take into account the cost of rebuilding a devastated land. The second Gulf War, over a decade later, cost far more.

- **refugees.** War forces thousands, sometimes millions, of people to leave their homes and, often, their countries as well. This turns them into refugees, people without a home. In 2001, there were thought to be over 12 million refugees in the world. The families of some Palestinian Arabs, dispossessed when the State of Israel was formed in 1948, are still refugees almost 60 years later.

- **economic cost.** War, inevitably, destroys homes, crops, water supplies, power supplies, industry, hospitals and schools. It costs millions of pounds to restore these supplies once the war is over. This uses up vast amounts of money that poor countries cannot afford. The developing countries of the world spend 22 times as much money on buying military weapons than they do on feeding their poorest citizens.

Work

1. What is a war?
2. Into which *three* groups can wars be divided? Write a short paragraph about each of them.
3. Describe *one* change that took place in the way that war was fought in the 20th century.

C.6 THE JUST WAR

KEY QUESTION What is a Just War?

Since the Second World War ended, there has barely been a time when there hasn't been an armed conflict somewhere in the world. It is very important, therefore, that you understand the different reasons why people go to war. It is also important that you look at one attempt that has been made to justify much conflict – the **Just War** theory.

Why do people fight?

There are many reasons why people go to war and some of them are better than others. They might fight to:

- defend their country against an aggressor. This was the major reason for the Second World War. Most people would argue that this is an acceptable reason for fighting.
- defend an ally that is under attack.
- defend a country's beliefs, religion or way of life.
- overthrow a country's leader or government (a civil war).
- remove a dictator or to stop genocide that is taking place in another country. Genocide is the attempt to wipe out a group or a tribe in a country. It is sometimes called 'ethnic cleansing'.
- expand territory or win control over important assets such as water or oil.

The conflict in Northern Ireland in the 20th century was fought for religious and sectarian reasons, but no one seriously suggested that it was a Just War in any sense.

The Just War theory

This attitude to war has a very long history. War can never be right but it might be, on occasions, less wrong than not going to war. If a war needs to be fought, then the Just War theory attempts to make sure that it is fought according to certain 'rules'. It was the Dominican friar and Church Father St Thomas Aquinas (1225–1274) who laid down the basic conditions for a Just War to which more were added later:

Condition 1: The war must be declared by the head of a country.

Condition 2: There must be a just cause for the war. In practice, this can only happen when a country is attacked and needs to defend itself.

Condition 3: The war must have a clear aim and this must be to advance good and not evil. The fighting must stop once the aim has been achieved.

Condition 4: Every other possibility for solving the conflict must have been tried before a war is declared, including extensive negotiations.

Condition 5: The war must be fought in a just way. This means that:
- certain weapons will be outlawed because they are inhumane.
- only as much force is used as is necessary to achieve victory.
- no violence must be directed against civilians.

The Just War theory is Christian in origin. The other religions, however, largely agree with its emphasis. Guru Gobind Singh, one of the Ten Sikh Gurus, taught that it is permissible to draw the sword when all other attempts to solve a situation have failed (Extract A). The Qur'an teaches that those who have been wronged have Allah's permission to fight – and Allah will give them victory. The jihad is an important Muslim belief. The Buddhist holy book, the Dhammapada, teaches that a great man is one who hurts no living thing, not someone who is a warrior and kills others. All religions allow force to be used in self-defence or when people are under threat.

> **EXTRACT A**
> "When all other means have failed, it is permissible to draw the sword."
> [Guru Gobind Singh]

KEY WORDS

Allah – Guru Gobind Singh – Jihad – Just War – Qur'an – Ten Gurus

EXAM TIPS

When you are dealing with a topical subject – such as abortion or war – it is always good to be able to introduce recent statistics or examples that you have found for yourself. Keep your eyes and ears open.

Work

1. Describe the conditions laid down for the fighting of a Just War.
2. Write down *five* reasons why people fight wars.

C.7 THE HOLY WAR AND PACIFISM

KEY QUESTION What is a Holy War?

It is a curious truth but religion and war have often gone hand in hand. In Topic C.6, we saw how the idea of a Just War was created to keep war within strictly-controlled limits. Here, we look at the notion of a Holy War and one response of many religious people towards war – that of pacifism. A Holy War is one in which God is claimed to be on one side, giving that side the final victory.

Below are three examples of Holy Wars from history:

The Israelites in the Holy Land

In the 13th century BCE, the Israelites were led by Moses out of Egyptian slavery and taken towards their Promised Land of Canaan. After the Israelites had crossed the Red Sea and the waters had come together to swallow up the Egyptians, Moses led the people in a song of triumph (Extract A). As you will see, the implication of these words is very clear. God is the supreme 'warrior' who has given a mighty victory to his Chosen People.

> **EXTRACT A**
> "I shall sing to the Lord, for he has risen in triumph; horse and rider he has hurled into the sea… The Lord is a warrior; the Lord is his name. Pharoah's chariots and his army he has cast into the sea…"
> [Exodus 15.1–2]

Constantine and the crusades

The Roman Emperor, Constantine, saw God in much the same light. Having won a victory against overwhelming odds, he insisted that a standard carrying the symbol of a cross went before his army into every subsequent battle. Centuries later a similar standard preceded the armies of the Christian Crusaders as they fought against the 'infidels' or 'pagans' who had occupied the Holy Land. Responding to a sermon by the Pope, they believed:

- they were fighting for a holy or noble cause.
- they were being led into battle by God.
- God was on their side because they were on His. It followed, then, that the opposing soldiers were the enemies of God.
- they should destroy everything in their path in the name of God.

We can see here all the elements of a Holy War. Any soldier who believes this will willingly surrender his life. For soldiers fighting in the Crusades, the assurance by the Pope that, if they died, they would have immediate eternal life was the only promise that they needed. In recent years, the same assurance of divine assistance has led many Muslim terrorists to sacrifice their lives as suicide bombers.

Pacifism

A pacifist is someone who does not believe that there is any situation which justifies a nation going to war. They believe that violence is always wrong in every situation. They may have religious beliefs which lead them to believe this – there is a strong pacifist tradition in both Christianity and Buddhism. Pacifists may not hold any particular religious beliefs but have arrived at this conclusion for other reasons. This is not an easy position to hold when a country is at war and many people quickly classify them as cowards.

In a time of war, many pacifists register as 'conscientious objectors'. In the First World War, some 16,000 people registered as conscientious objectors and this number had risen to almost 60,000 by the time of the Second World War. The Roman Catholic Church, which does not have a strong tradition of pacifism, teaches its members that if they cannot fight, they must offer themselves for other duties instead. In the two World Wars conscientious objectors often found themselves on the front line carrying out non-combatant duties, such as ambulance driving and stretcher bearing.

▶ There has always been a strong link between religion and war. Many people find this very difficult to understand.

Key Words

Just War – Moses – Roman Catholic Church – Pope

To Talk About

"Conscientious objectors are simply cowards by another name." Do you agree with this statement? If you disagree, how would you argue against it?

Work

1. Describe *two* Holy Wars.
2. What is a Holy War?
3. What are conscientious objectors?

C.8 What are Prejudice & Discrimination?

KEY QUESTION Why do prejudice and discrimination exist in the 21st century?

In this topic we are going to look at the third of our life issues – prejudice and discrimination. We will look at the differences between prejudice and discrimination and the ways that the different kinds of prejudice can affect our everyday lives.

It is hoped that, as black and white children grow up together, so they will learn to be less prejudiced.

What are prejudice and discrimination?

Prejudice. Prejudice means forming an opinion and judging a person, or group of people, on inadequate or incorrect information. It may be because of their race, sex, sexual orientation, colour or age. It is an opinion which will have been formed without adequate information and so will be largely based on ignorance or a misunderstanding of the facts.

Prejudice can be a very serious matter. During the Second World War (1939–1945), six million Jews were put to death by the Nazis in Europe. This prejudice against the Jews was built upon the totally false notion that they 'watered down' the pure Aryan nation that the Nazis wanted to build – and which would give them world domination. They also held the same opinion of gypsies and **homosexuals** – both of whom suffered greatly at their hands.

Discrimination. Discrimination is prejudice in action. It takes place when an individual or a group is singled out for less-favourable treatment than other people. Any form of discrimination – racial, sexual or any other form – is now illegal in this country. All religions are opposed to discrimination, although almost all religions have been guilty of it in the past and some still practise it today – such as discrimination against homosexuals and women.

> **TO TALK ABOUT**
>
> If you had the power to take one step to reduce the amount of prejudice and discrimination in the modern world, what would that step be?

Reasons for prejudice and discrimination

There are four main reasons why prejudice and discrimination are still facts of life in the 21st century:

1. **Fear.** In the 1950s, there were few black people in the UK but so many British men had been killed in the Second World War that Britain began to advertise in the Caribbean and elsewhere for labour. As a result, many black people came to Britain to live and they soon began to bring over their families to join them. Largely, black communities were established in many inner-city areas and white people began to feel threatened. Racial tension resulted. People began to fear for their own way of life and black people were blamed. There were race riots in parts of London and elsewhere based on a fear of the unknown.

2. **Ignorance.** The early part of the 21st century saw the birth of Islamophobia – a fear of Islam and Muslims. This was due to the activities of some terrorists who claimed a loose allegiance to Islam. This fear was not based on the facts or on an understanding of Islam. People made little effort to find out the truth about the religion.

3. **Upbringing.** Most of our prejudices are inherited from our parents. Many of the older generation are prejudiced against people of different religions, skin colour or sexual orientation. Comments that betray this prejudice are made in the home. Children grow up to believe that these opinions are normal and so they do not question them when they are older. They then pass on their prejudices to their own children and so on…

4. **Stereotyping.** We might base our attitude to another person or group on what we think that group is like – whether or not our assessment of them is correct. We then transfer to that group all the unpleasant characteristics that we think they have. In the past, for instance, the violence in Northern Ireland has led to people believing that all Irish people are violent. Of course, we know that such a picture is totally false, but that does not stop some people from believing it. Stereotyping can be very dangerous. It resulted in the Second World War in the deaths of millions of people.

In the topics that follow we are going to look at the prejudice and discrimination that manifests itself as racism (Topic C.9), sexism (Topic C.10), ageism, disability discrimination, religious discrimination and discrimination based on sexual orientation (Topic C.11).

Key Words

Ageism – Homosexual – Racism – Sexism

Work

1. a) What is prejudice?
   b) Give your own *two* examples of prejudice.
2. a) What is discrimination?
   b) Give your own *two* examples of discrimination.

C.9 Racism

KEY QUESTION What is racism and why is it illegal?

EXTRACT A
"*All human beings are born free and equal in dignity and human rights… human beings should act towards one another in the spirit of brotherhood; that everyone is entitled to all the rights and freedom… without distinction of any kind.*"
[Universal Declaration of Human Rights]

Racism is the belief that a person's nationality or skin colour should determine the rights and the opportunities that are given to them. As we shall see below, it is against the law to discriminate against anyone in this country in any way because of the colour of their skin. This does not mean, however, that such discrimination does not take place. It is notoriously difficult to prove that someone has lost a job opportunity or the chance to rent a flat because they are black. Britain is now a multi-racial and a multi-religious society.

Immigration

From the mid 1950s, immigrants began to enter Britain in large numbers in search of work or to escape persecution in their home country. The government of Britain was very pleased to welcome them because there was a marked shortage of labour in many industries because of the Second World War, when thousands of workers had been killed. The British Nationality Act of 1948 had given British citizenship to anyone born in a British colony.

This influx of immigrants was halted by the Commonwealth Immigrants Act of 1968 which allowed entry to British passport holders only if they were born, adopted or registered in Britain or had naturalised British parents or parents in one of those categories. This law was mainly passed to keep out East African Asians who were being persecuted in Kenya and Uganda – and wanted to make their home in Britain.

Today, there are about 2,500,000 black people living in Britain. They form about 4%, one in every 25, of the total population. Most of them were born in this country. To protect them, two Race Relations Acts have been passed:

1. **Race Relations Act (1968).** This made it illegal to discriminate against anyone because of their country of origin in the areas of employment, housing or education.
2. **Race Relations Act (1976).** This Act set up the Commission for Racial Equality to help people who suffered from racial discrimination at the hands of other people.

TO TALK ABOUT
Do you think it is true to say that young people are less racially prejudiced than the generations of their parents and grandparents?

KEY WORD
Racism

Racial discrimination

Racial discrimination is outlawed in four areas of life:

1. **Employment.** When black immigrants came to Britain in the 1950s and the 1960s, they were encouraged to fill largely unskilled or semi-skilled jobs. The evidence available shows that the vast majority of black people occupy the same kind of occupations today. Black people are heavily under-represented in managerial jobs and jobs of responsibility.
2. **Education.** A report in the mid 1950s found that black children and young people were under-performing at all levels in education – from primary through to university levels. The reasons were partly down to the attitudes of their teachers, who expected far less of them than their white counterparts. There are few black teachers to challenge these racist attitudes.
3. **Housing.** Black people have always suffered badly in the housing market. This is particularly true in the inner-city areas where most of them live and most of the housing is rented. It has left them wide open to discrimination by white landlords with property to rent out.
4. **The Social Services.** Black people make far less use of the social benefits available than white people. They are either not aware of them or are afraid to claim them. Many immigrants still speak imperfect English and this is a major obstacle in the way of them claiming benefits.

While prejudice and discrimination still exist in this country, the attitudes of people seem to be changing slowly. Surveys show that young people are much less prejudiced than their parents. There is still a long way to go, however, before racism is eradicated altogether.

This man holds a responsible post in education. Gradually, the number of black people in such occupations in this country is growing. ▶

Work

1. Describe *three* ways in which it is clear that Britain is now a multi-racial and a multi-religious society.
2. Describe how black citizens of the UK might suffer in each of the following areas:

    a) Education.
    b) Employment.
    c) Housing.
    d) Social Services.

C.10 Sexism

KEY QUESTION What is sexual discrimination and why is it outlawed?

Sexual discrimination and the law

Sexism takes place every time a person, usually a woman, is discriminated against in any area of life because of their sex. The Sex Discrimination Act of 1975 makes it unlawful to discriminate against anyone on the grounds of their sex in the areas of recruitment for a job, promotion at work and training. Job advertisements must not discriminate in their language, but they can make it clear that they are looking for people of a particular sex. If, though, a person of either sex applies, they must be treated equally and fairly.

Until the early 1990s, women could not become priests in the Church of England. They cannot yet become bishops. They still cannot become priests in the Roman Catholic Church.

Two exceptions were noted by the Act:

1. Women are not allowed to work underground.
2. Women may be debarred from the priesthood in any Church if they believe that a male priesthood is a 'Genuine Occupational Qualification' (GOQ).

This law came at the end of a long process by which women were gradually recognised as being equal with men:

- 1882 – women allowed to own property in their own right.
- 1892 – women allowed to vote in local elections.
- 1918 – women allowed to vote in Parliamentary elections at the age of 30.
- 1928 – women allowed to vote at the age of 21 – the same age as men.
- 1970 – women could not be paid less for doing the same job as a man.

Sexual discrimination in practice

There remain important inequalities between men and women in the UK today. Here are some of them:

- Parents are likely to lay down different rules for girls than boys – and to treat them differently.

- In education, girls are more likely to out-perform boys at GCSE, although the balance is restored at 'A' level.
- Women are much more likely than men to be the victims of domestic violence.
- Even if they are working full-time, women are much more likely than men to do most of the housework. Women are more likely than men to give up work to look after the home and children. Although there are exceptions, this is a role that makes most men feel uncomfortable.
- After a divorce, women are much more likely than men to gain custody of the children and this limits their chances of finding paid employment. On the other hand, it limits the access of most men to their children.
- Although more and more women are in paid employment, their salary levels are significantly lower than those of men. Women earn, on average 75% of what men earn. Nine out of every 10 part-time workers are women. Women are less likely to gain promotion and only about 10% of managers are women.
- Women are much more likely than men to experience poverty. One of the poorest groups in society is single mothers. There are about 1,200,000 single mothers in the UK.
- Nearly all of Britain's six million 'carers' are women. This form of work is called 'invisible' because it is largely unpaid and is often combined with outside employment.

Two explanations have been put forward to explain this inequality:

1. **The nature argument.** Men and women are different biologically and so they will act differently. Women are naturally the people to stay at home and care for the children because they are genetically programmed to do this.

2. **The nurture argument.** Men and women carry out different roles in society because this is what they have been taught to do. Young girls help their mothers around the home, while boys spend time with their fathers doing more 'masculine' work. In this way, girls learn that their principal role in life is as a homemaker, while boys learn that they are mainly responsible for bringing money into the family.

KEY WORDS

Church of England – Roman Catholic Church – Sexism

TO TALK ABOUT

Do you think that we live in an unfair society? Give examples to prove your point. What changes would you like to see to make society fairer?

Work

1. Give *four* examples of changes in the law in the UK over the past century to make men and women more equal.
2. Give examples from *three* different areas of modern life to show that men and women are still treated unequally.

C.11 Other kinds of prejudice

KEY QUESTION What other kinds of prejudice are there in our society?

Apart from racism and sexism, there are four other kinds of modern discrimination:

1 Ageism

Ageism is discrimination directed against people because of their age. The largest group of people needing help and support in the UK are the elderly. There are around 11 million people over retirement age (60 for women and 65 for men), 18% of the total population, of which:

- 52% live with their husband or wife.
- 36% live alone.
- 7% live with their children.
- 5% live in old peoples' homes.

The problems of growing old are mainly associated with failing health, poverty and loneliness. An increasing number of the elderly now find themselves facing a problem with their occupational pension as they get older.

2 Disability

According to government figures, 6.2 million adults and 360,000 children suffer from a disability of some kind. This includes mental handicap (such as Down's syndrome), mental illness (such as phobias, autism and schizophrenia) and physical handicaps (such as blindness, deafness or loss of a limb). The vast majority of people with a physical handicap do not need extra support, but many do. In 1981, the United Nations declared an International Year of the Disabled and made five promises:

1. To do whatever is necessary to allow the mentally and physically disabled to live a full life.
2. To support all efforts to train disabled people and to give them full employment opportunities.
3. To encourage public places to make access for disabled people a priority.
4. To educate the able-bodied about the needs of the disabled.
5. To prevent disability as much as possible and to help in the rehabilitation of those who are disabled. 60% of all disabled people live in developing countries where little help is available.

EXTRACT A
"*Mentally handicapped people have so much to give; they share our common humanity and like us all, are children of God.*"

[Church of England Report, 1984]

3 Sexual orientation

Homosexuals still experience discrimination against them. Although some homosexuals prefer to be called 'gays', others find that it is still used as a term of abuse by many people. It is illegal for someone to be discriminated against because of their sexual orientation, but such discrimination is still common. In the UK from December 2005, however, gay couples were able to go through a ceremony which legally recognised them as partners. So, for example, when a gay couple have lived together they can each inherit each other's pension rights if one of them dies. Many religions, however, still discriminate against homosexuals.

Many elderly people live the last years of their life in poverty and loneliness.

4 Religious prejudice

For a long time, Jews have found that their synagogues and cemeteries have been attacked with graffiti in areas which have a high Jewish population. Gravestones have been overturned and desecrated. After the destruction of the Twin Towers in New York in September 2001, Muslims have also found themselves the victims of religious prejudice in this country and overseas. Mosques have been daubed with graffiti and broken into. It is an offence to commit blasphemous acts against Christian and Jewish targets but not, as yet, against other religions. An attempt to remedy this situation was being made in 2005.

KEY WORDS

Ageism – Homosexual – Mosque – Racism – Sexism – Synagogue

TO TALK ABOUT

If you could make one change in society which would improve the lives of the elderly and the disabled, what would it be?

Work

1. a) What do you think are the basic needs of disabled people?
   b) Do you think that enough attention is paid to meeting the needs of the disabled?
2. Explain how and why people might be discriminated against because of *two* of these things: race; sexual orientation; age; disability.

C.12 Religious attitudes to prejudice

KEY QUESTION What are the attitudes of the different world religions to prejudice?

In common

The teachings of the major world religions have much in common. In particular, they teach that:

- all human beings are equal because this is the way they were created. This means that they have equal value in God's sight – although Buddhists do not believe in God.
- each person has the right to live and work freely and to find their own way to peace and happiness in the world. Human beings should treat other people with justice – equally and within the laws of each country. They also have the right to expect that other people will treat them in exactly the same way.
- even when there are differences between the different religious communities, tolerance and harmony should be maintained between them. Members of the different communities must respect the beliefs and practices of others.

The teaching of Buddhism

The sangha is made up of monks, nuns and ordinary people who are trying to pursue the Buddhist way of life. Those who belong to the sangha are pursuing generosity, kindness and compassion in the hope that they can reach enlightenment. In the enlightened state there is no distinction between male and female. It is in the sangha that Buddhists find the help that they need to live a moral life, and an important part of this is living in harmony with all human beings.

The teaching of Christianity

In the Bible, God created all people to be equal in His own image. Jesus treated Gentiles (non-Jews) and women the same as Jews and men (Extract A). Both Jesus and Paul declared that the kingdom of God was open to all people – its members are those who love one another and treat each other with care and respect.

> **EXTRACT A**
> "…There is no difference between Jews and Gentiles, between slaves and free people, between men and women; you are all one in union with Christ Jesus."
>
> [Galatians 3.28]

The teaching of Hinduism

The teaching of Hinduism strongly emphasises that everyone, human and animal, should be treated with the greatest respect because all have been created by God. This is important because it creates good karma and this continues forward and affects the next rebirth.

The teaching of Islam

Allah created all people equal. They are also different, although this should never be used to justify any prejudice or acts of discrimination. All Muslims, male and female, can reach Paradise, although members of other faiths will not. Under no circumstances should Muslims show prejudice or discrimination in their dealings with others. Fairness must be extended to all. The worldwide community of Muslims, the Ummah, expresses true unity.

The teaching of Judaism

Judaism has always had a long tradition of welcoming the stranger and the traveller. Those who seek help should always find it (Extract B). The prophets said that it was important that everyone within Israel should be treated with fairness and equality.

> **EXTRACT B**
> "...show love for those foreigners, because you were once foreigners in Egypt."
> [Deuteronomy 10.19]

The teaching of Sikhism

Sikhism teaches that everyone is a child of God and so should be treated equally. As all religions worship God, so all must be treated with the same respect. The equality of all people is expressed by the communal kitchen in the gurdwara, called the langar. Here, a meal is shared by all, Sikh and non-Sikh, after a service to express the true brotherhood of all.

◀ At the end of their service, Sikhs meet together in the langar, the kitchen linked with the gurdwara, to eat a meal together. Everyone is invited to express the Sikh belief that all people are equal in the sight of God.

KEY WORDS

Allah – Bible – Gurdwara – Jesus – Karma – Langar – Paul – Prophet – Sangha – Ummah

TO TALK ABOUT

Why do you think that the religions of the world have been responsible for maintaining some of the worst prejudice – against women and homosexuals, for example?

Work

1. What do all religions believe about prejudice and equality?
2. Describe what *two* of the religions you have studied believe about prejudice and equality.

EXAM QUESTIONS

Question 1 – Abortion
1. Write down *three* reasons why a woman might decide to have an abortion.
2. How do you think a woman's religious beliefs might help her to make her mind up about an abortion?
3. a) What is meant by the phrase 'the sanctity of life'?
   b) Do you agree that life is sacred?
4. List *three* reasons why someone might be opposed to abortion.
5. List *three* reasons why someone might support abortion.
6. "Abortion had to be made legal in 1967 with all the back-street abortions that were going on." Do you agree with this statement? Give reasons for your answer, showing that you have considered more than one point of view.
7. At the moment, only the woman has the right to be involved in the decision about an abortion. Do you agree or do you think the father should have a right as well?

Question 2 – War
1. How can the cost of war be measured?
2. How would you describe the attitude of the religion(s) that you have studied towards war?
3. What do religious people mean when they speak of a 'Just War'?
4. How do you think a religious person might argue that they are a pacifist?
5. What do religious people mean by a 'Holy War'?
6. "If there is a war, it is a cowardly position to be a conscientious objector." Do you agree with this statement? Give reasons for your answer, showing that you have considered more than one point of view. Refer to religious teaching in your answer.

Question 3 – Prejudice
1. a) List *four* reasons for the existence of prejudice in the 21st century.
   b) Which of the reasons you listed in a) do you think best explains why there is still prejudice today?
2. How might a person's religious beliefs convince them that racism is wrong?
3. a) What is racism?
   b) Describe *four* areas of life in which racism is now illegal in this country.
4. a) What is sexism?
   b) Which *two* explanations have been put forward to explain inequalities between men and women?
5. a) How can society discriminate against disabled people?
   b) What do you think are the *three* most important things that could be done to help disabled people?

Section D
Planet earth

In this section you will find out about:

D.1–2   The creation stories and teachings from the major world religions

D.3   What we can learn from the creation stories

D.4   Science, religion and creation

D.5   The responsibility that human beings have for animals

D.6–7   Vegetarianism

D.8   The use of animals in scientific experimentation

D.9   Blood sports

D.10–11   The damage that human beings are doing to the planet

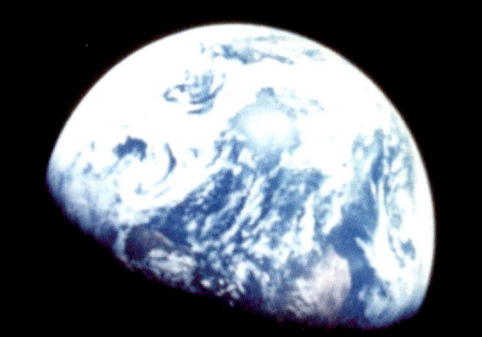

D.1 IN THE BEGINNING (1)

KEY QUESTION What is the teaching of Buddhism, Christianity and Judaism about creation?

Almost from the beginning of time, people have wondered about the answers to two questions – 'Where did the world come from?' and 'Where did I, and other human beings, come from?' Some of the oldest parts of the different holy scriptures try to provide answers to these two questions. In Topics D.1 and D.2 we will look at the answers supplied by the different religions.

Buddhism and creation

There is no creation story in Buddhism. The Buddha himself refused to speculate on how the world began. He was much more concerned about human suffering and what could be done about it. He simply did not believe that there was anything that could be said about creation that would help people to live better or more satisfactory lives. Buddhism teaches that the world evolves and follows the cycle of birth, life and death.

Christianity, Judaism and creation

Christians and Jews share the same creation story because they partly share the same scriptures – which Jews call the **Tenakh** and Christians call the Old Testament. The book of Genesis, the first book in the Tenakh/Old Testament, begins with two separate creation stories which underline that the universe was made by God out of nothing (Extract A).

▲ The Jewish and Christian creation story places the responsibility for the first sin and disobedience of God on the shoulders of Eve. She gave in to temptation and then persuaded the man to do the same.

EXTRACT A

"*When God began to create heaven and earth – the earth being unformed and void, with darkness over the surface of the deep and a wind from God sweeping over the water...*"

[Genesis 1.1–3]

118

In two stories that are over 3,500 years old, Genesis describes how God created the earth in six 'days' or periods of time before resting Himself on the seventh day. The stories do not go into any detail, they simply declare that God 'spoke' and the different parts of the universe and the created world came into being:

Day 1: Light

Day 2: The sky – described as a dome that separated the water above from the water below the sky.

Day 3: The waters were gathered together to form the seas with land appearing, and many kinds of plants.

Day 4: The sun, the moon and the stars (described as lights in the sky).

Day 5: The creatures in the sea and birds.

Day 6: All animal life and the first humans. The man and the woman were told to be fertile and fill the earth, exercising control over all other forms of life. They were a special creation by God and given pride of place in the Garden of Eden. Most importantly, they were made 'in the image of God' and this made them different from the rest of creation.

Day 7: God finished the work of creation and rested. This was the origin of the Jewish day of rest, Shabbat (the Sabbath Day).

Everything was perfect in the garden until the first man (Adam) and woman (Eve) deliberately disobeyed God. For this disobedience, they were thrown out of the garden and sin entered the world. The man was punished by having to work hard to tame the earth so that it would provide food for him and his family. The woman was punished by having to pass through the pain of child-bearing to populate the earth.

Key Words

Adam – Buddha – Old Testament – Shabbat (Sabbath Day) – Tenakh

Work

1. Why is there no creation story in Buddhism?
2. How does the creation story in Genesis describe the sequence of events that make up God's creative activity?
3. How does the creation story in Genesis end?

To Talk About

Why do you think that the Genesis creation story is insistent that God made the world 'out of nothing'?

D.2 IN THE BEGINNING (2)

KEY QUESTION What is the teaching of Hinduism, Islam and Sikhism about creation?

Although it does not have a creation story as such, Islam does have something important to say about creation. Sikhism does not have a creation story either but, again, it teaches some important truths about the creative activity of God. As there are many Hindu holy books, so there are several creation stories.

Hinduism

There are enough references in the different Hindu holy books to suggest that the world was originally made out of nothing. They suggest that a contemplation of the created world will leave the worshipper lost in wonder and amazement. If that happens, then it does not matter whether we know exactly how creation took place or not. This is very much the approach of Buddhism as well – a religion which has strong links with Hinduism.

Two main Hindu creation stories:

1. A hymn called the Purusha Sukta gives us the myth in which a great 'cosmic' man (Purusha) is sacrificed so that the world could be created. Different parts of Purusha were then used to make different parts of the universe (see Extract A).
2. A popular creation myth describes the god Vishnu, who was sleeping on a cobra snake that was floating on the ocean. Vishnu was woken up by the humming sound 'AUM' and a lotus flower grew out of his navel. The creator god, Brahma, was sitting on the lotus flower and Vishnu ordered him to break the flower into three parts – to make the heavens, the earth and the sky. Brahma then made the rest of creation – the grass, the trees, the birds, the fish, etc. Finally, he made people.

Islam and creation

The Qur'an does not give us a story about how the world was created, but it does teach that Allah created the world and everything in it. Human beings are the most important part of God's creative work and they have been created so that they alone can serve Allah. Although Allah controls everything in his creation, he has made human beings the 'guardians' of the earth. Responsibility for the day-to-day care of the earth has been delegated to the Muslim community (the Ummah).

EXTRACT A
"*His mouth became the Brahmin; his arms were made into the Warrior; his thighs the People, and from his feet the Servants were born. The moon was born from his mind; from his eye the sun was born. Indra and Agni came from his mouth and from his vital bread the wind was born.*"

[Purusha Sukta 12.13]

Muslims and Sikhs believe that people can find God in the most beautiful aspects of nature – both large and small.

The six 'days' of creation from the Jewish/Christian creation story finds an echo in the Qur'an. The Qur'an also accepts the statement in the Bible that man (Adam) was created before woman (Hewa) and that everyone is descended from these two original people. This is repeated twice in the Qur'an in passages that bear a close similarity to the early chapters of the Bible.

Sikhism and creation

There is no creation story in the Sikh holy book, the Guru Granth Sahib. For billions of years, the sun and moon; the earth and heaven; the day and night; the dark and light; the wind and waters; and even the gods did not exist. It was only the one Lord who existed. It was God who created the universe, the planets, the earth and the sky, the gods and human beings. He created everything out of nothing and in this way demonstrated His supreme power over all things.

God is not part of the creation that He has brought into existence. Yet, God is to be found within the created order. As Sikhs are keen to emphasise: "God is beyond all forms, yet is within all forms."

We can find evidence for God within the world that He has created. We may find out a great deal about God, and His creation, but our understanding is always limited because we are limited in our understanding. Only God is infinite and unlimited. Fortunately, God has chosen to reveal a great deal that we could not know otherwise.

Key Words

Adam – Allah – AUM – Bible – Brahma – Guru Granth Sahib – Qur'an – Ummah – Vishnu

To Talk About

Is there any place for God when you think about how the universe, the world and human beings were created? If so, where do you think He is to be found?

Work

1. Describe *two* Hindu creation stories.
2. List *three* things that Islam teaches about the relationship between Allah and creation.
3. What does Sikhism teach about God and creation?

D.3 WHAT CAN THE CREATION STORIES

KEY QUESTION
What 'truths' are underlined by the teachings of the different religions on creation?

The different religious creation stories are among the oldest stories in existence. They do not tell us very much, if anything, about the actual way that the universe, the world or human beings began. As religious myths, however, they make important points about us as human beings and our relationship with the universe in which we live. In particular, they teach that:

1 God created the world

The Jewish/Christian creation story opens with the words: "In the beginning, when God created the universe…" (Genesis 1.1). Athough most of the other holy books do not have a creation story, they assume that it was God who created the universe, the earth and all forms of life. It follows from this that the world belongs to God. This is God's world. Human beings are, at best, His caretakers.

2 Human beings are God's stewards

In the Genesis account of creation (chapters 1 and 2), we discover that, after each of the six days of creation, God is said to have looked at what He had created and saw that it was 'good'. God is described as being very pleased with His creative handiwork. The same story makes it clear that God's creation, symbolised by the Garden of Eden, was originally perfect. So perfect, in fact, that it does not seem that the first man and woman even had to work for their food. It was there, ready to hand, for them to take and enjoy.

From the beginning, however, human beings were expected to be the stewards of God's creation. A 'steward' is someone appointed by his master to look after something that is very precious to him. Muslims prefer to use the word 'guardian' (khalifah) to describe the relationship which God always intended between human beings and the world that He created. This idea has three important implications. It means that it is humankind's responsibility to:

- take care of the earth. Human beings have the responsibility of caring for the world and keeping it in good condition. Buddhism teaches very strongly that everything, including the most insignificant creatures, should be cared for and cherished without a single one of them being harmed. Buddhist monks put this into practice by carrying a strainer with them so that the water they drink will not contain any creature that they may swallow by accident.
- protect the earth. This includes protecting those parts of nature that cannot protect themselves – the animals, the birds and the fish, as well as the mountains, the seas and the rivers. Hindus believe that the universe is sacred and precious. They believe it to be part of God. It is, therefore, the duty (dharma) of every person to care for all living creatures so that they can build up good karma.

The world of nature can only survive if human beings protect it.

- enjoy the earth and all that it provides. Most creation stories make it clear that it is God's intention that the earth should be fruitful, and so meet all the needs of human beings. It is the teaching of Islam that human beings have a responsibility of looking after the world because in that way they are showing the respect that they have for Allah.

Why looking after the planet is important

On a human level, it could be argued that looking after the world now is desperately important because we have a duty to hand it on to our children in a healthy condition. That is right and that is part of what the holy books teach. It is in our own interests to make sure that the universe is not harmed. Many religions teach that a Day of Judgement is coming when all people will stand before God to account for the way that they have lived.

One of the issues on which this coming judgement will be based is the way that all of us have treated the world in which we live. The Qur'an makes it clear that the Ummah, the worldwide Muslim community, has been given the heavy responsibility for maintaining the health of the planet. If Muslims wish to enjoy eternal life spent in the presence of Allah, they must have fulfilled this responsibility fully. Otherwise, they will be sent to hell.

Key Words

Allah – Dharma – Karma – Qur'an – Ummah

To Talk About

What might people today take from the different creation stories, even if they do not accept that they tell us anything about the way that the universe was created?

Work

1. What do the many creation stories teach above everything else?
2. What are *three* implications of describing human beings as God's stewards on earth?
3. Why do religious people believe that it is very important to look after the earth?

D.4 Science, religion and creation

KEY QUESTION What does science tell us about the origins of the universe and human life?

Since the holy texts of the different religions were written thousands of years ago, scientists have discovered a great deal about the origins of the universe and life on earth. This knowledge has transformed the way that we look at life and our place as insignificant human beings in the universe. This raises many questions about the accounts of creation that we find in the holy books.

1 The place of human beings

Nicolaus Copernicus (1473–1543) was a Christian priest and an amateur astronomer. Until the 16th century, people believed that the earth was at the centre of the universe – with the sun, the moon and the stars acting as lights in the heavens to light up the earth. The whole universe was believed to revolve around the earth. This was important for religious reasons as human beings were thought to be at the centre of God's creation. Copernicus upset many people when he declared that the earth was just one of billions of planets in one of millions of solar systems. He said that our solar system travelled around the sun and not the other way round. In terms of the whole universe, the earth is very small and insignificant, making human beings even less important.

2 The origins of the universe

In the 17th century, James Ussher, the Archbishop of Armagh, used the Bible to date the creation of the world to 4004 BCE by working his way back through the many genealogies in the Bible to its opening chapter. We now know, of course, that the universe is about 18 million years old. Most scientists believe that everything started with a Big Bang, an explosion that led to plasma flying through the universe at terrifying speeds. The effects of this Big Bang are still being felt in the outer reaches of the universe. The explosion eventually led to the formation of galaxies and these are still moving away at great speed from the centre of the explosion. As the galaxies travel through the universe, so they cool and slow down. It is the cooling of the gases that has led to the formation of stars and planets, including the earth.

3 The origin of life on earth

The theory of evolution was the most important scientific breakthrough of the 19th century. This was a far greater challenge to religion than the work of Copernicus. The theory is associated with Charles Darwin, who spent some years on the Galapagos Islands studying plant and animal life. His work convinced him that all life evolved (developed) over a very long period of time. As life grew, so it adapted itself to its surrounding conditions (called 'natural selection'). Only the strongest species could do this – the weakest died out (called the 'survival of the fittest'). Darwin described nature as being 'red in tooth and claw' in this battle to survive.

Nature is 'red in tooth and claw'.

Many people at the time were worried that this was a direct challenge to the teachings of the Christian religion. They were far more worried, however, when Darwin said that evolution not only applied to plants and animals but also to human beings. Christians had always thought that human beings were unique and made in God's image – now Darwin said that they were simply animals.

Science and religion

Religion is, of course, much older than science. As we have seen, many holy books have their own myths, or stories, to explain how the world and human beings were created. It is natural that many people should conclude that science and religion have little to say to each other. Two interesting thoughts, however, might challenge this conclusion:

1. Science and religion deal with different aspects of experience. Science deals with facts and how they should be understood. These facts have to be discovered first and then investigated. To investigate them, we use our five senses – seeing, hearing, touching, tasting and smelling. Religion deals with spiritual 'facts' which are understood by faith. To understand life fully, we need both the scientific and the religious approach.
2. Religions claim that the world was created by God and is based on laws that He set in place. Science believes that its task is to discover those laws and then begin to understand them. Science and religion could be two sides of the same coin. This is why many scientists are also religious believers.

Key Word

Bible

To Talk About

In 1999, the 'Today' programme on BBC Radio 4 invited listeners to name 'the most significant British figure of the second millennium'. Almost everyone mentioned Shakespeare and Churchill but there was barely a mention of a scientist. Does this surprise you?

Work

1. Why do you think that the word 'revolution' is used to describe the work of Nicolaus Copernicus?
2. What do scientists mean when they talk of the 'Big Bang'?
3. What is meant by the theory of evolution?

125

D.5 Human beings and animals

KEY QUESTION How do the major world religions understand the relationship between human beings and animals?

In this topic we will be looking at the different attitudes of our religions to animals and their place in creation. Most religions agree that animals occupy a lower place in the plan of God than human beings – that animals were intended by God to provide human beings with food.

> **EXTRACT A**
> "*We are not masters of this earth. It belongs to God and He has entrusted us with its safekeeping. His trustees are responsible for maintaining the unity of His creation, its wildlife and natural environment.*"
> [Assisi Declaration]

Buddhism and animals

Each part of nature depends on another for its health. The animals depend on the health of plant life. Human life depends on the health of animal life. Each part of nature is also part of the cycle of reincarnation. The First Precept of Buddhism – "I will not harm any creature" – covers the whole of nature. It is wrong to harm any form of life – even the smallest and most insignificant.

Christianity and animals

The story of creation in Genesis makes a very important point. The birds, animals and land creatures were all created by God on the fifth day, but human beings were created a day later. This is because human beings are different to animals. This is shown in two ways:

1. Human beings, but not other animals, are created 'in the image of God'. Only human beings bear a spiritual likeness to God. They, alone, are capable of worshipping Him.
2. In the Garden of Eden, man was given the task of naming all the animals and this was an ancient way of showing his power over them. Man was placed in charge of the animals. They would provide him with food as long as he carried out his responsibility of caring for them.

Hinduism and animals

Hindus and Buddhists respect animals more highly than the followers of any other religion. Many Hindus believe that they have been animals in previous reincarnations and may well reappear as one in a future rebirth.

The cow is a sacred animal for all Hindus.

They believe that all forms of life are related to each other because all life is part of Brahman (God). This is why protecting animals is part of a Hindu's dharma (duty). Almost all Hindus believe that the cow is sacred because of its links with the god, Krishna, who was a cowherd when he visited earth.

Islam and animals

Muslims believe that the whole of creation is a unity. One part depends on another and the whole is beautifully balanced by Allah. If the health of one part is damaged, then the health of the whole is affected. God has promised that nature will supply all that human beings need as long as they look after the world properly. All animals and insects are part of that world – no matter how small and insignificant they are. The Prophet Muhammad ﷺ often spoke of planting trees and gardens from which animals, as well as humans, could benefit. By respecting animals, humans are respecting Allah.

Judaism and animals

In the Jewish scriptures, owning animals was very important to every Jew because it was their work in the fields that provided food for every family. For this reason, it was essential that animals were cared for properly. This was recognised in the Ten Commandments. On the Sabbath Day, it was not only humans who needed to rest – the animals were also given a day off! Oxen and donkeys were mentioned, in particular, since they were beasts of burden.

Sikhism and animals

Sikhism teaches that human beings are superior to animals but this does not mean they can be mistreated. Human beings should always be kind to them. Sikhs believe in reincarnation. In any future reincarnation they will be judged, in part, on the way that they have treated animals. Ideally, human beings and animals should work together (Extract B).

EXTRACT B
"*The Lord pervades all created beings: God creates all and assigns all their tasks.*"
[Guru Granth Sahib 434]

KEY WORDS
Allah – Brahman – Dharma – Krishna – Muhammad ﷺ – Prophet – Reincarnation – Sabbath Day – Ten Commandments

TO TALK ABOUT
Do you agree that animals occupy a lower place in creation than human beings and that their main purpose is to provide humans with food?

Work

1. What do Buddhists believe about the interdependence of all parts of creation?
2. How do people who believe in reincarnation stress that animals are lower down the scale than human beings?

D.6 Vegetarianism (1)

KEY QUESTION What is vegetarianism?

It is thought that, in this country, one in every 10 people follows a vegetarian diet. This means that they do not eat any meat. A much smaller proportion of people are vegans – they do not eat any product that comes from animals, e.g. dairy products such as eggs.

▶ Buddhist priests with their begging bowls.

Reasons for being a vegetarian

There are several possible reasons why a person might be a vegetarian. It might be because:

- it is healthier to eat only vegetables – especially if they have been grown organically without being exposed to pesticides.
- their religion encourages them to be vegetarian. Although vegetarians can belong to any religion, most Hindus and Buddhists are vegetarians because of the encouragement that their religion gives them to adopt this lifestyle.
- they have been brought up in a vegetarian household and have never acquired the taste for meat.
- they are unhappy about modern farming methods, and the ideas of factory farming and slaughtering animals make them feel very uncomfortable.

In this topic we are also going to look at the guidelines in Buddhism and Christianity about diet and the food that people should eat. Neither of these religions teaches that there is a strong link between diet and religious commitment – unlike Islam and Judaism. In other words, it is possible to eat meat and still be a good Buddhist or Christian.

Buddhism and food

One of the basic principles of being a Buddhist is that one's lifestyle should not harm any living creature (ahimsa). This principle, which Buddhism inherited from its close early relationship with Hinduism, extends to all living creatures. Most Buddhists in this country believe that accepting this principle means adopting a vegetarian diet and lifestyle.

The principle, however, is not necessarily accepted in other Buddhist countries. Buddhist monks, for instance, obtain their food and other necessities by standing out with their begging bowls. They will accept gifts of meat if they are offered to them and eat the meat without any difficulty. They will not, however, kill the animals themselves for food. They are reminded that, at the time of the Buddha, eating meat was normal. At the same time, they know that in killing an animal they could be killing the body that houses one of their ancestors.

Christianity and food

There are many Christians who are vegetarians, although they were probably not prompted to become one by their religious faith. They became vegetarians for other, largely humanitarian, reasons. They believe, for instance, that slaughtering animals for food is cruel or that many animals are raised under cruel conditions.

In the Genesis story of creation, there is no encouragement for the first human beings to eat meat, although they are told: "I have provided all kinds of grain and all kinds of fruit for you to eat…" (Genesis 1.29). As far as the animals and the wild birds are concerned, we are simply told that God has provided all that they need to eat. After the Flood, however, God gave permission for human beings to eat animals for food with the one proviso that they should not eat meat that contains blood (Extract A).

Christian vegetarians receive no encouragement from the life or teaching of Jesus. He had little to say about food or diet, although we are told that he shared a fish meal with his disciples after he had risen from the dead.

EXTRACT A
"*Every creature that lives shall be yours to eat; as with the green grasses, I will give you all these. You must not, however, eat flesh with its life-blood in it.*"

[Genesis 9.3–4]

TO TALK ABOUT
The rule against eating meat which contains blood is found in both Islam and Judaism. Why do you think it was considered to be so important in ancient times?

EXAM TIPS
You may be asked for a personal opinion on vegetarianism. You will be expected to argue for one side or the other, while showing that you are aware of the opposing point of view.

KEY WORDS
Ahimsa – Buddha – Jesus

Work

1. Describe *four* reasons that a person might have for being a vegetarian.
2. a) What is ahimsa?
   b) What is the link between ahimsa and many Buddhists' decision to be vegetarian?
3. What guidance is given in the Bible about the food that a person can eat?

129

D.7 Vegetarianism (2)

KEY QUESTION What is the teaching of the different religions on vegetarianism?

Of the four religions considered in this topic, Hinduism has a strong vegetarian tradition and Sikhism only serves up vegetarian food in its regular communal meal each week in the langar. While there are vegetarian Muslims and Jews, there is nothing in their religious teaching to encourage this.

Hinduism and food

Hinduism teaches reincarnation, with animals being an essential part of the cycle of birth, death and rebirth. The Vedas, a very important Hindu holy book, makes it clear that all meat should be avoided because it breaks a fundamental teaching of Hinduism – ahimsa – that Hindus should be completely non-violent. As it is completely impossible to kill an animal without being violent, so eating meat is ruled out. Even if a Hindu is not a vegetarian, eating any part of the cow is ruled out because cows are sacred animals.

Islam and food

Few Muslims are vegetarian and meat is part of most Muslim diets. It must, however, be halal meat which has been killed in a certain way and: "…in the name of Allah, the merciful, the compassionate."

Halal meat can only be obtained from animals that are slaughtered by having their throats cut with the blood then being totally drained out. The Shahadah must be pronounced over the animal before it is killed. Muslims and Jews agree that only white meat is acceptable to eat. They also agree that no product taken from a pig can be eaten, although any products taken from cows, sheep and poultry are acceptable.

EXTRACT A
"*Eat of the good and lawful things which God bestowed on you, and give thanks for God's favours if you truly serve Him.*"
[Qur'an surah 16.114]

Judaism and food

Like Muslims, Jews also have strict laws based on the teachings of their holy book – the Torah. These rules date from the time when the ancestors of the Jews were travelling away from slavery in Egypt across the wilderness. The rules that they were given then about diet (called kashrut) are still followed by most Jews today. The method by which all acceptable animals are killed (called **shechita**) must be humane, with the animals being stunned before they are slaughtered by a single strike across the throat from a very sharp knife.

A halal shop. Only animals that are killed according to strict rules are considered fit for Muslims to eat.

Extract B summarises which animals are acceptable for Jews to eat. Food that is acceptable is called kosher. Meat is perfectly acceptable as long as it is cooked separately from dairy produce. In strict Jewish households, separate saucepans are kept for this purpose. Any product of the pig is forbidden.

Sikhism and food

Although most Sikhs do follow a vegetarian diet, some eat meat (Extract C). It is only vegetarian food, however, that is served in the langar, the communal kitchen that is attached to every gurdwara. A meal is produced in the langar as a service is going on so that everyone can sit down to eat together once the service has finished. It is normal for everyone at the service to stay for this. To accommodate the needs of everyone, this meal is always vegetarian. If a Sikh eats meat, then the animal must have been bred and killed humanely.

EXTRACT B
"…You may eat any land animal that has divided hoofs and that also chews the cud… Do not eat pigs. They must be considered unclean; they have divided hoofs but do not chew the cud. Do not eat these animals or even touch their dead bodies; they are unclean."

[Leviticus 11.2–3, 6–8]

TO TALK ABOUT

Why do you think most religions consider that the food people eat has a spiritual, as well as a physical, importance?

KEY WORDS

Ahimsa – Allah – Gurdwara – Halal – Kashrut – Kosher – Langar – Reincarnation – Shahadah – Shechita – Torah – Vedas

EXTRACT C
"All food is pure, for God has provided it for our sustenance."

[Guru Granth Sahib 472]

Work

1. What is the link in Hinduism between reincarnation and vegetarianism?
2. What are the rules that have to be carried out before an animal becomes halal meat?
3. What makes food kosher and acceptable for Jews to eat?

D.8 Vivisection

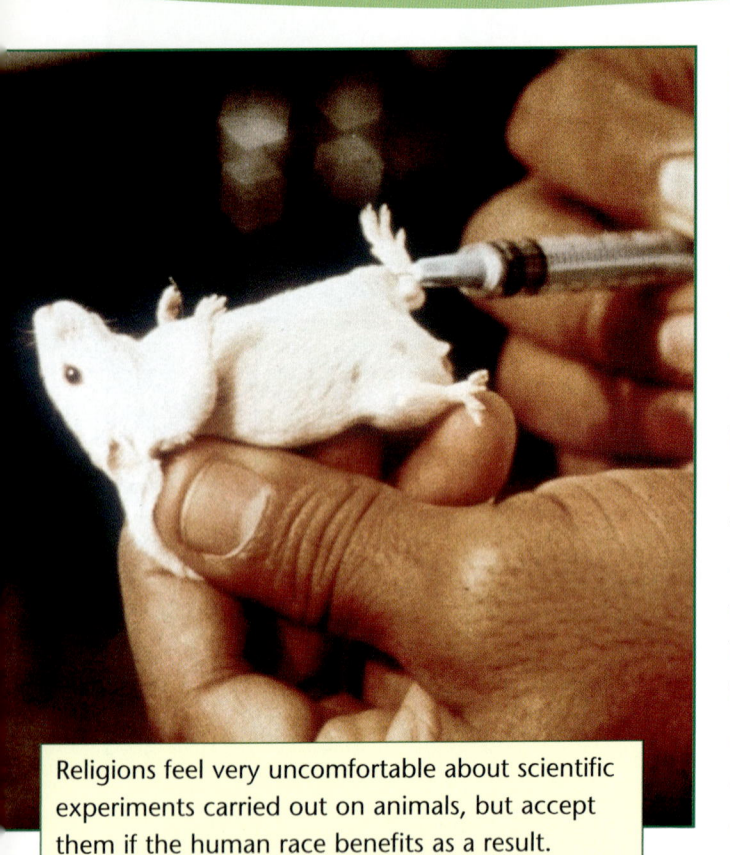

KEY QUESTION What is vivisection and what is the attitude of the major world religions to it?

Carrying out scientific experiments on animals (called **vivisection**) is highly controversial, arousing strong feelings in many people who are opposed to it. There can be no doubt, however, that such experiments have been important in the past – leading to vaccines against such killer diseases as diphtheria, polio and rubella. At the same time, it has also been used to test for new and better cosmetics and toiletries which could also be carried out using computer simulation and cell-culture. This has led many people to question whether scientific experiments on animals are still necessary.

Religions feel very uncomfortable about scientific experiments carried out on animals, but accept them if the human race benefits as a result.

Buddhism and vivisection

Buddhists believe that all of nature depends upon each other for its health. If one part of nature is misused, then the whole of creation will suffer as a result. This means that no single part of nature is free to use or misuse any other part. Buddhists are totally against the use of animals in medical research – even if human beings benefit as a result.

Christianity and vivisection

All of the Churches believe that experiments carried out on humans for essential medical research are acceptable and necessary. The value of animal life is less than that of human life. Even if such work is necessary, however, it should always be carried out humanely. Trivial experimentation for cosmetics is totally unjustified.

The Roman Catholic Church warns its members not to give too great an importance to animals. Many people are suffering a great deal in the world and our attention should be focused on them. Our approach to animals, including pets, should be sensible. Quakers, however, are strongly opposed to animal testing.

KEY WORDS

Allah – Murti – Quaker – Roman Catholic Church – Vivisection

Hinduism and vivisection

The Laws of Manu, an important Hindu holy book, expresses the Hindu belief that all life is sacred – insects, birds, animals, fish and human beings. The gods and animals are often placed together on a murti. Hindus do not feel happy about the use of animals in scientific experimentation. They are opposed to any unnecessary experimentation and any use of animals that causes them considerable pain. At the same time, if such experimentation is essential, and there is no alternative, then it is acceptable.

Islam and vivisection

If animal experimentation is important in the battle against disease, then it is acceptable. This is based on the simple principle that human life is much more important than animal life. Anything else is an offence against Allah (Extract A).

> **EXTRACT A**
> "A good deed done to a beast is as good as doing good to a human being: while an act of cruelty to a beast is as good as an act of cruelty to a human being."
> [Hadith]

Judaism and vivisection

Jews are told by their scriptures not to cause any pain to the animals for which they are responsible. If experiments on them are the only way to lift future human suffering, then it is acceptable, but no unnecessary suffering can be caused.

Sikhism and vivisection

Sikhism holds a similar position to the other religions – animal experimentation is only permissible if human life will benefit in the long term. Human beings may be superior to animals but that gives them the responsibility of treating them with care. Since it is God who creates animals, it is also God who decides how they should be treated (Extract B).

> **EXTRACT B**
> "The Lord pervades all created beings: God creates all and assigns all their tasks."
> [Guru Granth Sahib 434]

> **TO TALK ABOUT**
> Most religions teach that experiments on animals are acceptable as long as human beings benefit in the end. Do you agree with this? Bring some arguments forward to justify your conclusion – whatever it is.

Work

1. Why are Buddhists totally opposed to the use of animals in scientific experimentation?
2. What is the position of Christianity on vivisection?
3. Do Judaism and Sikhism agree about vivisection? Explain your answer.

D.9 Hunting and other blood sports

> **KEY QUESTION** Why do blood sports, especially hunting, arouse such strong feelings?

When most people refer to 'blood sports' they are usually referring to:

- hunting.
- shooting.
- fishing.

A 'blood sport' is one in which the intention of the activity is to spill the blood of an animal, whether or not it is designed to bring about its death. Each of these three activities, or 'sports', arouses strong feelings in people, although it is the issue of hunting foxes and deer with horses and hounds that has gained most attention in recent years.

Hunting

It is, of course, true to say that people have hunted animals almost since time began. There is, however, one important difference between the hunting that ancient people engaged in and hunting today. In times past, people needed to hunt and trap out of necessity for food whereas, in recent years, people have hunted as a sport. Although hunting still goes on in some parts of the world so that families and villages can be fed, increasingly it has become an activity that people do mainly for their own enjoyment and exercise. Supporters of hunting, however, have always argued that it also plays an important part in conservation by reducing the number of foxes and deer to more manageable levels.

The decision by a Labour Government to commit itself to the abolition of hunting when it was elected in 2001 was very controversial. The abolition of fox and deer hunting in England and Wales was finally introduced at the beginning of 2005:

- Those opposed to fox hunting were delighted and say that there are much more effective ways of keeping the number of foxes under control. They also maintain that a chase followed by hounds tearing a fox apart is very cruel and completely out of place in the modern world. This satisfies a basic 'blood lust' in human beings and people should not be allowed to participate in such a barbaric sport.
- Those who support fox hunting maintain that it is an important part of the tradition of the countryside. It provides employment for a large number of people. Foxes do have to be controlled and they suggested that some form of licensing hunts would have been better than abolishing it altogether. They lost the argument.

> **TO TALK ABOUT**
>
> What are your own opinions about blood sports? How would you justify those opinions?

Almost all religions are against the idea of hunting for pleasure. The holy books were written long before this idea became popular and they do occasionally allow that hunting for food may be a necessity (Extract A). It is always accepted that the needs of human beings are more important than those of animals.

> **EXTRACT A**
> "*If someone kills a sparrow for sport, the sparrow will cry out on the Day of Judgement, 'O Lord! That person killed me for nothing. He did not kill me for any useful purpose!*"
> [Muslim Hadith]

Shooting

Shooting birds for sport is very popular in some parts of the country – especially on large country estates. People pay large amounts of money to become part of a shooting party. The birds – mainly pheasants and grouse – are bred especially for the shooting, which can only take place at certain times of the year. 'Beaters' go ahead of those with the guns, driving out the birds so that they can be shot. The birds are then sold to be used in restaurants or simply eaten by those who shoot them. Some people, lovers of wildlife, find this quite barbaric, although, because it takes place well away from the gaze of the public, there is little organised opposition to it.

Fishing

Fishing is the most popular of all sports in this country. It is estimated that up to three million people fish either regularly or occasionally. Fishing competitions are held on lakes, rivers and in the sea. Sometimes the fish are kept and eaten, but they are usually thrown back so that they can grow larger. Some people believe that fishing inflicts pain on the fish but supporters insist that the fish feels little, if any, pain. There seems no way of discovering the truth.

▶ Hunting foxes with hounds was made illegal in the United Kingdom in 2005.

Work

1. What is meant by a 'blood sport'?
2. In the argument about hunting that raged in the early 21st century, what were the main arguments put forward by those who supported, and opposed, hunting?
3. Why might some people be against:
    a) shooting?   b) fishing?

D.10 Damaging the planet (1)

KEY QUESTION Why are deforestation, global warming and destroying the ozone layer three of the greatest problems facing the planet?

The word 'environment' refers to the planet on which we live and the atmosphere surrounding it. The environment is suffering greatly from the effects of pollution brought on by misguided human activity and behaviour. Here, we are going to look at three examples of the damage that we are causing to our environment – deforestation, global warming and the destruction of the ozone layer.

Deforestation

Deforestation refers to the permanent clearing of forest, especially rainforest, areas for agriculture or settlement. Between 1985 and 1995, forest areas throughout the world were cleared at the rate of over 40 million acres a year – and the clearance rate has speeded up since then! Forests are now being cleared at the rate of an area the size of Great Britain every week. An area the size of a football pitch is cleared every second! This is extremely serious because:

- deforestation makes a considerable contribution to global warming. Carbon dioxide is the most important of the greenhouse gases which build up in the atmosphere and cause global warming (see below). These gases trap heat warming the earth and about 20% of carbon dioxide comes from the burning of the forests.
- although rainforests only cover 6% of the earth's surface, they contain 50% of all the earth's species – plants, insects, animals, etc. About 5,000 different species a year are being lost. Many of them have not even been named yet! Many life-saving drugs come from plants that only grow in forest areas.
- rainforests are essential for regulating the climate and limiting flooding. In the Venezuelan mud-slides, which killed thousands in 1999, deforestation was a major factor. The trees in the forest areas bound the earth together before they were uprooted and burned – with disastrous consequences.

Global warming – the greenhouse effect

EXTRACT A
" ...do not destroy the trees; the trees are not your enemies."
[Deuteronomy 20.19]

Our planet is surrounded by a blanket of gases which insulates it and guarantees a steady temperature in which life can survive and prosper. This blanket acts like a greenhouse around the earth but, because of pollution (see Topic D.11), the greenhouse is becoming too warm. A build up of carbon dioxide in the atmosphere is trapping the heat radiated by the earth.

TO TALK ABOUT

Are you optimistic or pessimistic when you look at the future prospects of the human race?

During the last 100 years, the overall temperature of the earth's surface has risen by almost 1%. This may not sound a lot but, if it continues, it will mean that the ice-caps in the Antarctic and Arctic Oceans will melt and the water levels in the oceans will rise by about 1.5 metres – meaning that many low-lying inhabited parts of the world will be flooded by water.

The ozone layer

Ozone in the atmosphere, formed from a small amount of oxygen, forms a layer above the earth. This filters out the lethal ultraviolet rays from the sun. Over the years, the use of chlorofluorocarbons (CFCs) in such appliances as fridge compressors and aerosols has led to the destruction of ozone molecules in the upper atmosphere. These chlorine compounds remain active in the atmosphere for at least 100 years, even though the use of most of them has now been phased out. The holes which these compounds have punched in the ozone layer will take a century, or more, to repair. In the meantime, people on earth are vulnerable to a whole range of health hazards from eye cataracts and skin cancer to crop damage.

The destruction of rainforests is one of the major threats to the environment.

EXTRACT B

"*For too long we have thought of the atmosphere as a limitless good. We have been burning fuel and emitting pollutants, pressing aerosol buttons and blowing foam to our heart's content… The time has come to develop an action plan for protecting the atmosphere… Time has come to start the process of change… For too long we neglected that we have been playing lethal games with vital life-support systems.*"

[Gro Harlem Brundtland, Norwegian politician]

EXAM TIPS

You will find more in the newspapers about pollution and environmental matters than almost any other topic. Make your own collection of material on this and other social topics to use in your examination answers.

Work

1. What is global warming?
2. What is the ozone layer and what does it do?
3. How rapidly are the rainforests being destroyed?

D.11 Damaging the planet (2)

KEY QUESTION How serious is the pollution of the environment?

◀ A recent study showed that Bath was one of the most polluted areas in Britain. It also showed that the health of the people living there suffered a great deal because of the pollution.

In Topic D.10 we looked at three major environmental problems – deforestation, global warming and damage to the ozone layer – which affect people across national borders. In this topic, we look at pollution on a more local level – although such pollution, and its effects, cannot be confined to one country.

Air pollution

In 1955, there were about 40 million cars in the world but at the beginning of the 21st century that number had increased to over 400 million. It is estimated that by 2025 there will be over 1,000 million cars in the world. Cars are a major source of pollution for two main reasons:

1. Hydrocarbons are released from petrol, and sunlight acting on them produces low-level ozone. This ozone affects the breathing of millions of people, causing coughing and choking. It is a major cause of asthma, affecting, in particular, children under the age of 5. This is particularly bad in city centres for obvious reasons.
2. Other dangerous pollutants in petrol can cause cancer, reproductive problems and birth defects. Lead in the air can cause learning difficulties for young children of primary school age.

Waste pollution

The average British household disposes of a tonne of rubbish each year. Most of this rubbish is placed in landfill sites but much of it is not biodegradable. By doing this, therefore, we are polluting the earth and leaving future generations to deal with the consequences. Recycling is the only real option for the future.

Water and land pollution

For thousands of years, humanity consigned much of its waste to rivers and seas. As long as the waste materials could decompose naturally and there was enough water to wash them away, little long-term damage was done. But as cities have grown, and industry has increased, so the toxicity of waste material has become so much greater. Many rivers have lost their natural ability to clean themselves as pollution has increased.

In recent years, large quantities of pesticides and nitrates have been used on farmland in Britain to make the ground more productive – and more resistant to pests. Rain has washed these off the land and into local rivers and streams. Fish have been killed in their thousands, poisoned or suffocated. Drinking water has often been badly affected.

All of these forms of pollution have had a drastic effect on wildlife. So has the loss of many very valuable habitats. Since 1945, the UK has lost many of its most valuable habitats: hedgerows (150,000 miles); wildflower meadows (95%); and ancient woodlands (50%). Numerous species of plants and animals live in these specialised habitats – no habitats means no species.

The downward spiral

The overall picture is very worrying. The human race cannot continue to rush headlong down this path without suffering severe consequences. The whole of the planet's fragile future depends on maintaining the balance between the health of the earth and the needs of its inhabitants. Much of the answer must lie in humankind being willing to change the way it lives and behaves. It must begin to live in harmony with nature – not against it.

However, more than this is needed. Both governments and industry must change the way that they think of the earth and its resources. These resources are finite (limited). They will soon run out. As you will see in Extract A, this present generation is obliged to hand on to the next generation the world in as pure a condition as possible.

EXTRACT A
"*We have not inherited the earth from our fathers, we are borrowing it from our children.*"
[Lester Brown, American environmentalist]

TO TALK ABOUT
What do you think are the major problems that face the environment in the United Kingdom? What do you think should be done about them?

Work

1. Describe *three* major causes of pollution.
2. Why is the disposal of waste such a major problem in the modern world?
3. Why are the rivers and streams of Britain becoming so polluted?

Exam questions

Question 1 – The earth
1. What does the religion(s) you have studied teach about the beginning of the universe and life?
2. What can we learn from the religion(s) you have studied about our responsibility for looking after the earth?
3. What does it mean to describe human beings as 'stewards' or 'guardians' of the earth?
4. What does the religion(s) you have studied teach about respect for the animal kingdom?
5. How does the Genesis story of creation stress that human beings and animals are different and should be treated as such?

Question 2 – Human beings and animals
1. What are the main arguments that people put forward for becoming vegetarians?
2. What takes place in the langar of a gurdwara and what is its significance?
3. a) What is vivisection?
   b) What is the attitude of the religion(s) you have studied to vivisection?
4. "Human beings are free to use animals in scientific experiments because they have been given control over them by God." Do you agree with this statement? Give reasons for your answer, showing that you have considered more than one point of view. Refer to religious teaching in your answer.
5. "God intended us to eat animals for food so there is no need to be a vegetarian." Do you agree with this statement? Give reasons for your answer, showing that you have considered more than one point of view. Refer to religious teaching in your answer.

Question 3 – Pollution and destruction of the planet
1. Why does global warming represent such a threat to the future of the planet?
2. Why is the ozone layer under threat?
3. Why are rainforests so important for the future of the earth?
4. What is the major cause of air pollution and what effect does it have?
5. What are the major causes of water and land pollution?

Glossary

Abortion The surgical removal of a foetus from a woman's womb. *94*

Abraham One of the founding fathers of the Jewish, Christian and Muslim faiths. His story is told in the book of Genesis and in some surahs of the Qur'an. *21*

Adam The first human being in the Jewish/Christian scriptures and the Qur'an. *80*

Adi Granth The sacred book of Sikhism, also known as the Guru Granth Sahib. *47*

Ageism Discrimination against a person because of their age. *112*

Agnostic Someone who is not sure whether or not God exists. *64*

Ahimsa The teaching of non-violence towards all living creatures in both Buddhism and Hinduism. *30*

Allah The name for God in Islam. *34*

Amritsar The holy city of Sikhism in the Punjab which houses the Golden Temple. *47*

Anatta One of the three characteristics of ordinary existence in Buddhism, along with anicca and dukkha. *10*

Anglican Church The name given to Churches throughout the world which follow the teachings of the Church of England. The third largest Church after the Roman Catholic and the Orthodox Churches. *22*

Anicca One of the three characteristics of ordinary existence in Buddhism, along with anatta and dukkha. *10*

Apostles' Creed A statement of Christian belief thought to have been drawn up at the end of the 4th century. *19*

Ardas The Sikh prayer that forms a vital part of every service. *52*

Arhat A Buddhist who has reached nibbana. *84*

Ark The cupboard in a Jewish synagogue which houses the scrolls of the Torah. *45*

Atheist Someone who believes that there is no God. *64*

Atman The eternal soul which is identical with Brahman in Hindu belief. *28*

Atonement The death of Jesus, which Christians believe brought them to be 'at one' with God. *20*

AUM The most sacred word of Hinduism, placed at the beginning and end of books and uttered before all prayers. Composed of three sounds, said to represent the Trimurti. *32*

Avatar An appearance on earth of the god Vishnu in Hinduism. *28*

Baptist Church A worldwide Protestant Church which believes in adult baptism and not infant baptism. *23*

Bhagavad Gita 'The Son of the beloved.' The most famous and popular of the Hindu scriptures. *27*

Bible The holy book of Christians which also includes the Jewish scriptures. *18*

Bismillah Phrase meaning 'in the name of God, the merciful, the compassionate' which prefaces every surah in the Qur'an except one. Essential part of every Muslim prayer. *35*

Bodhisattva Someone in Buddhism who has been enlightened but chooses to stay behind to teach others, rather than enter nibbana immediately. *70*

Book of Common Prayer The first prayer book of the Church of England, from the 16th century. *22*

Brahma The Hindu Creator God, member of the Trimurti. *9*

Brahman The Supreme God or Ultimate Spirit in Hinduism. *28*

Breaking of Bread Name given by some Protestant Churches to the service of Holy Communion. *25*

Buddha The title, meaning 'the Enlightened One', assumed by Siddattha Gotama after his enlightenment. *6*

Church The name given to a Christian place of worship. *19*

Church of England The Established Church in England. *54*

Covenant The special agreement made between God and the Jewish people during the time of Abraham. *40*

David One of the earliest, and the best loved, of Israel's kings. *40*

Dharma Word used in Buddhism to refer to the teachings of the Buddha, one of the Three Refuges. *10*

Divine Liturgy Name used in the Orthodox Church for the service of Holy Communion. *22*

Dukkha Important feature of Buddhist teaching, where it is the first of the Four Noble Truths, referring to the existence of suffering. *10*

Easter Sunday The day on which Christians celebrate the Resurrection of Jesus from the dead. *20*

Eightfold Path The eight steps which offer a Buddhist the path to finding an answer to suffering. *12*

Epistle A letter written by one of the early Christian leaders and included in the New Testament. *24*

Eucharist 'Thanksgiving', the name used in many Anglican churches for the service of Holy Communion. *24*

Exodus The journey of the Jews out of Egyptian slavery towards their Promised Land of Canaan. *40*

Five Ks The five symbols worn by Sikhs who belong to the Khalsa: kesh (uncut hair); khanga (steel comb); kachs (shorts); kara (steel bangle); and kirpan (short sword). *50*

Five Moral Precepts The five moral beliefs held by all Buddhists. *12*

Five Pillars The five basic beliefs on which Islam is based – a belief in God, prayer, fasting, giving alms and pilgrimage to Makkah. *38*

Four Noble Truths The set of principles through which Buddhists can reach enlightenment. *8*

Ganesha One of the most popular Hindu gods, has an elephant's head. *29*

Golden Temple The central temple of Sikhism, also known as the Harimandir, situated in Amritsar. *48*

Good Friday The day on which Christians remember the crucifixion of Jesus. *20*

Gospel One of four books in the New Testament which contains a record of the life and teachings of Jesus. *16*

Granthi Man or woman who looks after the Guru Granth Sahib in a gurdwara and offers regular readings from the holy book. *49*

Gurdwara A Sikh place of worship. *46*

Guru A teacher or guide in an Eastern religion. *26*

Guru Gobind Singh The last of the Ten Sikh Gurus. *47*

Guru Granth Sahib The holy book of Sikhism, replacing the human Ten Gurus. *47*

Guru Nanak The founder of Sikhism and the first of the Ten Gurus. *46*

Gutka A collection of some of the hymns that are found in the Guru Granth Sahib. *52*

Gyatri Mantra A Hindu prayer book. *32*

Hajj The pilgrimage to Makkah, one of the Five Pillars for Muslims. *39*

Halal Meat that has been killed according to rules laid down in the Qur'an and so is fit for Muslims to eat. *50*

Harimandir Name for the Golden Temple in Amritsar. *48*

Havdalah The service that ends the Sabbath Day for every Jew. *45*

Hijrah The migration of the Prophet Muhammad ﷺ from Makkah to Madinah in 622 CE, an event which marks the beginning of the Muslim calendar. *34*

Holocaust The killing of six million Jews by the Nazis in the Second World War. *80*

Holy Communion The service celebrated by almost all Christian Churches, at which bread is eaten and wine drunk to remember the death of Jesus. *24*

Holy Spirit The third member of the Christian Trinity, the gift of Jesus to his followers after he left the earth. *16*

Holy Week The week beginning with Palm Sunday and ending with Good Friday, during which Christians remember events in the last week of the life of Jesus. *20*

Homosexual A man or woman who prefers to have sexual relations with a member of their own, rather than the opposite, sex. *106*

Hukam In Sikh thought, the term for God's will, the cause of the creation of the world. *53*

Iblis The tempter in the Qur'an, allowed by God to tempt Muslims. *75*

Imam The man who leads prayers in a mosque. *38*

Incarnation Christian term to describe the birth of God in the person of Jesus. *18*

Israel The country of the Jews. *40*

Japji A Sikh hymn to be found at the beginning of the Adi Granth. *48*

Jerusalem The city which is holy to three religions – Judaism, Christianity and Islam – scene of many religious conflicts. *40*

Jesus The founder of Christianity. *16*

Jihad A holy war fought by Muslims in the name of Allah. *93*

Just War A war that many people seek to justify on Christian moral grounds. *102*

Ka'bah The Islamic shrine in Makkah which is at the centre of Islam and thought to have been built by Abraham. Muslims always pray facing in the direction of the Ka'bah. *34*

Kachs Shorts worn by members of the Khalsa. *51*

Karah parshad A mixture of flour, butter, sugar and water which is shared by Sikhs at the end of all ceremonies as a symbol of universal brotherhood. *53*

Karma The idea in Hinduism, also found in Buddhism and Sikhism, that believes every action performed now has an effect on a person's life in the next rebirth. *31*

Kashrut The Jewish code which states which foods are kosher – foods that may be eaten and how they are to be prepared. *45*

Kesh Uncut hair. According to the rule of the Khalsa, Sikhs must let their hair grow to its natural length as a mark of their spirituality. *51*

Khadijah The wife of Muhammad ﷺ. *34*

Khalsa The brotherhood for Sikh males and females, everyone wears the Five Ks as symbols of belonging. *50*

Kirpan Short sword worn by members of the Khalsa. *51*

Kirtan Hymns sung by Hindus in praise of God. *53*

Kosher Food that is permitted by the Jewish dietary laws, also includes rules about the way that food is prepared. *45*

Krishna One of the most popular Hindu gods, an avatar of Vishnu, and known for his sense of fun. *27*

Lakshmi The Hindu goddess of wealth, beauty and good luck, the consort of the god Vishnu. *29*

Langar The kitchen attached to every gurdwara, in which a vegetarian meal is prepared during a service and eaten afterwards. *53*

Last Supper The last meal that Jesus shared with his disciples before he was crucified and the pattern for Holy Communion. *24*

Liturgy Public worship in a church which follows any prescribed order of service. *22*

Lord's Supper The name given to the service of Holy Communion by some Protestant Churches. *25*

Madinah The second sacred city of Islam, the place to which Muhammad ﷺ fled during the Hijrah in 622 CE. *34*

Madraseh The Muslim school at which children learn about their language and faith. *35*

Mahabharata A Hindu holy book. *27*

Makkah The birthplace of Muhammad ﷺ and most sacred city of Islam, the destination of the Hajj. *34*

Mala beads Beads used by Buddhists to help them meditate. *15*

Mandala Symmetrical diagrams, pictures and sculptures to represent the universe used in Hindu meditation. *32*

Mandir A Hindu temple. *26*

Mantra Hindu words or short phrases that are repeated continually during meditation to concentrate the mind. *14*

Mass The name given in the Roman Catholic Church to the service of Holy Communion. *25*

Messiah The leader that the Jews were expecting to lead them into freedom. *43*

Methodist Church One of the largest Protestant Churches. *54*

Mezuzah A small parchment scroll inscribed with two passages from the Torah and attached to most rooms in a Jewish home and the outside of the house. *72*

Middle Way Another name for the Eightfold Path in Buddhism – between extreme asceticism and a life of luxury. *12*

Mihrab The niche in the qibla wall of a mosque marking the direction of the Ka'bah in Makkah. *34*

Misbeha A string of 33 beads used by Muslims to help them to remember the 99 names of Allah. *36*

Missal The Prayer Book of the Catholic Church, including everything that a worshipper needs to play a full part in worship. *22*

Moksha Liberation from the endless cycle of birth, death and rebirth in Hinduism. *30*

Mool Mantra A Sikh chant. *48*

Moses The great Jewish leader who led the Jews out of Egyptian slavery and passed on the Ten Commandments to them. *40*

Mosque 'Place of prostration', the place of worship and prayer for Muslims. *34*

Muhammad ﷺ Muslims believe that Muhammad ﷺ was the last, and the greatest, of Allah's prophets. *34*

Mukti Same as moksha (see above). *73*

Murti Name given to an image of a Hindu god. *71*

Nam Used in Sikhism as a name for God. *49*

New Testament The second part of the Bible, containing four Gospels and letters from early church leaders. *21*

Nibbana Means 'to blow out', the blowing out of desire, and so is the indescribable state of bliss reached by the enlightened. *8*

Nicene Creed One of the earliest Christian Creeds (statements of belief). *19*

Nirodha The Buddhist term for the extinction of desire, means the same as nibbana. *11*

Old Testament The Jewish scriptures which were incorporated with the New Testament to form the Christian Bible. *21*

Orthodox Church Originally the Church of the eastern region of the Roman Empire, which separated from the western Church (the Roman Catholic Church) in 1054. *22*

Parable An everyday story told by Jesus containing an important spiritual lesson. *16*

Paul The most important leader of the early Christian Church and the writer of many books in the New Testament. *21*

Pentecost A Jewish festival, the day on which the Holy Spirit was given to the early Church. *19*

Peter A disciple of Jesus who is believed by Catholics to have been the first Pope. *21*

Pope Leader of the Roman Catholic Church, believed by Catholics to be the successor to Peter. *54*

Prophet Someone sent to deliver God's message to the people. *34*

Protestant Church A Church which is not Roman Catholic nor Orthodox. *23*

Puja A Hindu act of worship. *26*

Purgatory In Roman Catholic belief, the place to which souls go after death to prepare them for heaven. *89*

Quaker A Protestant Church which believes strongly that all life, human and animal, should be safeguarded. *23*

Qur'an The holy book of Islam, believed by Muslims to contain the revelations given to Muhammad ﷺ by Allah. *35*

Racism Discrimination against a person based on their nationality or the colour of their skin. *108*

Rama Hero of the Hindu epic, the Ramayana, he was one of the ten avatars of Vishnu. *29*

Ramadan The Islamic month set aside for fasting from food and drink during daylight hours, one of the Five Pillars of Islam. *39*

Ramayana Hindu epic from 5th century BCE which contains 24,000 verses. *27*

Reincarnation One of two major beliefs about life after death, held by Buddhists, Hindus and Sikhs. *31*

Resurrection One of two major beliefs about life after death, held by Jews, Christians and Muslims. *20*

Rig Veda The most sacred and ancient scriptures of Hinduism. *26*

Roman Catholic Church The largest of the Christian Churches, recognises the authority of the Pope. *22*

Rosh Hashanah The Jewish New Year, recalling the act of God in creating the world, beginning of 10 days of repentance ending with Day of Atonement. *44*

Rusulullah The Muslim belief that Muhammad ﷺ is unique as Allah's Prophet. *38*

Sacrament A special Christian service, such as Holy Communion, by which a spiritual blessing is given to the worshipper. *22*

Sacred Thread Hindu symbol of initiation for boys, hangs from left shoulder to right hip, boy is 'twice-born' after ceremony. *26*

Samsara Hindu and Buddhist term to denote the continual movement of the soul through birth and rebirth. *31*

Sangha The community of monks who follow the teachings of the Buddha. *9*

Sannyasin Hindu holy man. *68*

Satan 'The Accuser', the fallen angel opposed to God in Jewish and Christian belief. *75*

Sawm Term used in Islam for fasting, one of the Five Pillars. *39*

Sexism Discrimination against a person based on their sex, whether male or female. *110*

Shabbat (Sabbath Day) The Jewish day of rest, following the example of God who rested on the seventh day after creating the world. *44*

Shahadah Term used by Muslims for the confession of faith and the first Pillar. *38*

Shechita The Jewish laws relating to the slaughter of animals. *130*

Shema 'Hear', the Jewish name for the words of Deuteronomy 6.4, recited twice daily by Jews. *42*

Sheol The place of the dead in the Jewish scriptures. *86*

Shirk Term used in Islam for the sin of idolatry. *37*

Shiva The Hindu god of life, death and rebirth. *28*

Shofar The ram's horn trumpet blown in the synagogue at the services of Rosh Hashanah and at the conclusion of Yom Kippur. *44*

Shruti A group of the oldest Hindu scriptures, material which was 'heard' directly from the gods. *26*

Smriti Group of Hindu scriptures which were not given by the gods but 'remembered' from human tradition, contains some of the best-loved Hindu holy books. *27*

Surah A chapter or division in the Qur'an. *35*

Synagogue Jewish place of study, prayer and worship. *44*

Talmud A Jewish holy book which is the most important source of Jewish law. *97*

Tawhid Basic belief of Islam that God is one. *36*

Ten Commandments The 10 important Jewish laws given by God during the Exodus on Mount Sinai. *40*

Ten Gurus The 10 spiritual leaders whose teachings form the basis of Sikhism. *46*

Tenakh Name of the Jewish scriptures, made up of the Torah, the Writings and the Prophets. *118*

Theist Someone who believes in God. *64*

Three Refuges Statement by Buddhists that they take refuge in the Buddha; the dharma and in the sangha. *10*

Three Universal Truths (Marks of Existence) Term used in Buddhism for the three basic teachings of the Buddha. *10*

Torah The first five books of the Bible, the most sacred part of the Jewish scriptures. *40*

Transubstantiation The belief of Roman Catholics that the bread and wine turn into the actual body and blood of Jesus during the Mass. *25*

Treyfah Food in Judaism which is not kosher and has not been killed according to Jewish dietary laws. *45*

Trimurti The three main gods after Brahman in Hinduism – Brahma, Shiva and Vishnu. *28*

Trinity Basic belief of Christianity that God the Father, God the Son and God the Holy Spirit are the three Persons of the Trinity. Christians do not believe in three Gods. *18*

Ummah The worldwide community of Muslims. *39*

Upanishads A group of Hindu scriptures, thought to have been the result of disciples sitting at the feet of their gurus to be taught. *26*

Vedas The earliest collection of Hindu scriptures, dated between 1500 and 800 BCE. *26*

Vihara Term used in Buddhism for the monastic hall. *10*

Virgin birth The Christian belief that the father of Jesus was the Holy Spirit and not Joseph. *16*

Virgin Mary The mother of Jesus. *37*

Vishnu 'The preserver', the kindest of the Hindu gods. *28*

Vivisection The use of animals for scientific experiments. *132*

Waheguru Term chanted in Sikhism as part of meditation, means 'Wonderful Lord'. *49*

Writings One of the three divisions of the Jewish scriptures, including the book of Psalms. *41*

Wudu The washing ritual carried out by a Muslim before prayers. *38*

Yoga Used as a method of self-control and meditation in several religions. *33*

Yom Kippur The most solemn day in the Jewish year, the Day of Atonement, when the people repent for their sins. *44*

Zakah A payment from Muslims to help the poor and needy, the third Pillar of Islam. *38*